Christmas in The Netherlands

*Candlelight and quiet devotion warms
the homes of The Netherlands on
Christmas Night.*

*A kindergarten class in Eemnes
shares a candlelit banquet of Christmas treats* (cover photo).

Christmas in
The Netherlands

From World Book

World Book–Childcraft International, Inc.

A subsidiary of The Scott & Fetzer Company

Chicago London Sydney Tokyo Toronto

Staff

Editorial director
William H. Nault

Editorial

Executive editor
Robert O. Zeleny

Managing editor
Dominic J. Miccolis

Senior editor
Seva Johnson

Administrative assistant
Janet T. Peterson

Writer
Theresa Kryst Fertig

Researcher
Kathleen L. Florio

Crafts editor
Renée Mandel

Food Consultants
Tone Bergen
Ina Pinkney

Art

Executive art director
William Hammond

Art director
Joe Gound

Design director
Ronald A. Stachowiak

Senior designer
Free Chin

Production artists
Hans W. Bobzien
Susan T. Wilson

Photography director
John S. Marshall

Senior photographs editor
JoAnne Martinkus

Photographer
Steve Hale

Food stylist
Monique Hooker

Product production

Manufacturing
Joseph C. LaCount

Research and development
Henry Koval

Pre-press services
J. J. Stack

Production control
Barbara Podczerwinski
Janice M. Rossing

Composition
John Babrick

Film separations
Alfred J. Mozdzen

Editorial services

Director
Susan C. Kilburg

Editorial research
Mary Norton, head

Rights and permissions
Paul Rafferty

Text consultants
Robert D. Haslach
Assistant to the Counselor
for Press and Cultural Affairs
The Royal Netherlands Embassy
Washington, D.C.

Sheila C. Gazaleh-Weevers
Contributing editor,
Roaming 'Round Holland
Rotterdam, The Netherlands

The editors wish to thank the many associations and private individuals in The Netherlands and the United States that took part in developing this publication. We regret that there are so many, we cannot name them all. Special recognition, however, goes to the staff of The Netherlands Consulate-General at Chicago. Their encouragement and assistance were invaluable in all phases of the project.

Our appreciation also goes to the staff and students of The American School of The Hague, Elementary Division, for providing many schoolroom materials, including the illustrations on page 26. For research and translation assistance, we thank Edmée Pratt-de Ruyter de Wildt and Louisa M. Ruyter. For their special contributions in photographing Dutch foods, thanks go to Abraham Broersma and Ineke Phillips. Finally, we appreciate the assistance of Helen Heppard and Marcia Goodridge of Schuuring and Lang Associates for their assistance in obtaining delft and pewter for photography.

The story "The Three Skaters" (pp. 48–49) and the St. Nicholas songs (pp. 74–77) are adapted from *Santa Claus, The Dutch Way* (The Hague: Albani), with the permission of the Ministry of Foreign Affairs, The Hague.

"Er Is een Kindeke Geboren," "A Little Child Is Born" (pp. 78–79) is adapted from "De Nederige Geboorte," "The Simple Birth," arranged by Walter Ehret, words adapted from a Flemish/English translation by George K. Evans. From THE INTERNATIONAL BOOK OF CHRISTMAS CAROLS, copyright © 1963, 1980 by Walter Ehret and George K. Evans. Reproduced by permission of The Stephen Greene Press, Brattleboro, Vermont.

Contents

A Sinterklaas Parade

Sinterklaas! What mystery and magic surround the arrival of this white-bearded, robe-bedecked spirit of goodness. He is the herald of winter merriment for Netherlanders. In answer to the many Dutch hearts yearning for his appearance all year long, St. Nicholas, as Sinterklaas is also known, arrives well before his feast day December 6. Mid-November finds his steamer chugging through the canals of The Netherlands. Also aboard is the saint's swarthy companion, Zwarte Piet—Black Pete—a Moor. A fully costumed crew and the saint's famous white horse complete the group. They are said to have journeyed all the way from far-off Spain to prepare for St. Nicholas Eve. Called Sinterklaas-avond, it is the most beguiling night of the year for the Dutch.

Amsterdam, the capital city, hosts the good saint's official entrance into the country. He arrives aboard the steamer *Spanje,* the Dutch word for Spain. TV cameras are on hand to record the exciting event for the nation to view. But, at the same time, this wonder-worker is also making personal appearances in other towns and villages throughout the country.

He might dock again on the *Spanje,* or by almost any other kind of boat. He might arrive by helicopter, trolley, carriage, bicycle—even by taxi. On this day, he is all over The Netherlands at once. So will he remain through late December 5.

Excitement pulsates in Amsterdam Harbor as the steamer carrying Sinterklaas approaches. And the arrival of fun-loving Pete electrifies the celebration even more. Throngs of citizens young and old gather to greet the famous visitors, waving flags, shouting, and singing as with one voice:

Look, there is the steamer from faraway lands.
It brings us St. Nich'las, he's waving his hands.
His horse is aprancing on deck, up and down,
The banners are waving in village and town.

Sinterklaas' arrival was just as exciting years ago (above) *as it is today* (right).

Photographers and city officials get the first close view of Sinterklaas as he makes his way down the gangplank.

The steamer finally docks amid booming guns, ringing church bells, and cheering voices. The entire population of Amsterdam seems to have turned out for this festival. All ages and creeds, the rich and the poor alike are celebrating.

The event is without religious overtones, even though Sinterklaas wears the vestments of a bishop. Tradition has transformed him into a universal benefactor. It is everyone's pleasure to welcome the saint to The Netherlands.

As Sinterklaas and Pete disembark, the contrast between them is obvious. The saint is stately and all-forgiving. He has a beard and wears bishop's clothes. He is elegant in his white robe, crimson mantle, and tall red mitre as a headdress. His gloved hands are often adorned with jeweled rings, and he always carries a golden crosier, or staff, shaped like a shepherd's crook.

Pete, on the other hand, is a mischievous, grinning character dressed somewhat like a 16th-century Spanish page. He paints a comical picture in his long stockings, short, puffed britches, tight-fitting jacket, pleated collar, and plumed beret tipped over one ear. All are in bright, contrasting colors.

After the long-awaited pair alights from the steamer, Sinterklaas mounts his white horse, also elegantly adorned with trim of red and gold. On land, Sinterklaas always rides this brilliant—albeit nameless—steed. Youngsters believe this animal will carry Sinterklaas over the rooftops each night, listening down the chimneys with Pete to check on their behavior.

But today Sinterklaas and his horse are busy leading a magnificent parade. The youngsters have been waiting for what probably seems an eternity for this day to arrive. Many have, no doubt, coaxed their parents into bringing the entire family to the momentous event. Assuredly, though, little prodding is required to convince any Dutch person to join in the festivities. On occasions, there have been as many as three quarters of a million persons on hand in Amsterdam to greet Sinterklaas and Pete. The honored twosome experiences similar receptions in the other Dutch towns and villages where they disembark, as well.

Traffic is usually in a complete snarl. Streetcars come to a halt as conductors and passengers struggle to peek at the celebrities and the ongoing activities. Even the police have been known to forget their duties momentarily to cheer for St. Nicholas and Pete.

The weather at this time of the year is generally cold, damp, and dreary. Rather than depressing the population, however, it seems to cheer everyone. These bleak conditions are often referred to as "real St. Nicholas weather." There is not a soul who would prefer any other weather for the occasion. In fact, some say the drearier the day, the more *gezellig,* warm and cozy, the atmosphere.

Dutch flags fly from houses all along the route of the saint's triumphant ride. In Amsterdam, the spectacle often begins at St. Nicolaaskerk, or St. Nicholas Church, near the central railway station. It leads to Dam Square in front of the Royal Palace. Like mortal celebrities, Sinterklaas must occasionally be rerouted due to road repairs or other urban headaches.

The parade is an extravagant affair. There are balloons, brass bands, a cavalcade of children's organizations, acrobats, and other entertainers. A favorite parade entry of all youngsters is floats. These often depict fairy-tale scenes from familiar stories such as "Cinderella" and "Sleeping Beauty." Even characters like Donald Duck and the Flintstones occasionally participate.

Throngs of children line Sinterklaas' parade route through Amsterdam as he rides past on his brilliant white horse.

The mayor of Amsterdam officially greets Sinterklaas at the main square in front of the Royal Palace (right). "Real St. Nicholas weather" is overcast—even bleak. Some say the drearier the day, the cozier the atmosphere for the saint's appearance (below).

During the parade, Pete is especially delightful. Often there is a whole brigade of Petes surrounding or following Sinterklaas. They may number as many as 50. A group of these jolly figures might prance or dance along the parade route, telling jokes and handing out sweets to the children. "Petes" might also walk, cycle, or ride small, silly motor scooters. These puff, pant, and make ridiculous noises.

No matter what they may be doing, the "Petes" are never far distant from the saint. Often a group of students dressed like Pete will run around with sacks. The students pass out cookies and marzipan to each youngster in the crowd, enjoying their volunteer role in courtly costume. Whatever the case, this collective Pete adds unbounded mirth to the event.

In the cities, towns, and villages where Sinterklaas alights, local officials are always on hand to participate in the celebration. The mayor and others in his group frequently dress formally for the occasion in top hats and coats. They might greet Sinterklaas the moment he arrives. They then enthusiastically join in the parade, with St. Nicholas and his milk-white stallion in the lead. Often, a police motorcade and a big brass band will head them all. The route generally leads to a square adjacent to the town hall or to a large market place. There, the mayor presents Sinterklaas with an official welcome for all the gathered citizens to hear. In years past, the queen has attended the festivities in Amsterdam to add her greeting to the revered saint.

Also in Amsterdam, and elsewhere where the event is televised, a newscaster may corral Sinterklaas now for an on-the-spot TV interview. Whether watching in person or at home on their television sets, citizens are always eager to hear the saint's hallowed comments.

11

A tiny child's dreams come true when Sinterklaas picks her out from the crowd for a special greeting.

Then comes the time for the prestigious visitor to step to the podium and bestow some sage words upon the crowd at hand. Sinterklaas may begin by hailing the mayor and other town officials. He thanks them and the crowd in general for the warm welcome he and Pete have received. But Sinterklaas will probably be brief with these comments. He is eager to address those most important spectators who have been waiting so long and patiently: the children. He might tell them first how happy he is to be back in The Netherlands again after a year's time spent in Spain. Perhaps he will go straight to the

Young and old listen eagerly when-ever Sinterklaas makes a speech—this time, in front of a shopping center.

type of behavior he expects from them in the coming days. Whatever the topic of his words, they are not spoken in vain. The wee audience listens, firmly in the grasp of the stern but benevolent figure address-ing them.

Evident from watching the actions of this kindly character is how much he enjoys being among the children. They are equally elated finally to have him near. What luck, should they have the chance to shake his hand or touch his beard!

These little admirers have crowded along the en-tire parade route, craning their necks to catch a glimpse of the famous guest. Most fortunate are those perched on the shoulders of an adult, thus gain-

ing a better view. Sinterklaas is profoundly obliging. He never hesitates to stop and tweak a miniature nose or grasp a small, outstretched hand along the way.

Also customary from the good saint are whispered warnings into little ears about behaving during his stay. Sinterklaas may possibly stop to remind some children about their conduct records, which he has been keeping in his big, red book. He often reads from this carefully recorded log when out among his juvenile followers. It reveals his intimate knowledge of their year's activities, good and bad.

Some children are eager to rush to the saint for a short chat. Others, as can be expected, are a bit dubious about making direct contact with the immortal character. Sinterklaas can overlook a little shyness, however. He is a kind, tolerant parent figure who forgives everyone and who, above all else, loves every child.

During his discussions with the children, Sinterklaas might drop hints about the kind of snack his horse prefers. The youngsters need this information. They will be leaving just such a snack at night in a shoe, set near the hearth, in hopes of finding a treat from St. Nicholas the next morning. Dutch youngsters set out the enticements often between the parade and December 5. The take, of course, depends upon their past record and current behavior, which Sinterklaas and Pete will watch closely.

Though Pete is a marvelous character who thrills the children almost as much as Sinterklaas himself, he does so in a far different manner. Compared with the stately saint, Pete is quite the frivolous fellow, full of jollity and the oddest of antics. He jumps, hops, skips, and rolls his large eyes—sometimes blue, sometimes brown—to the children's delight.

Pete is known to carry with him one or more unique objects. The most important is that famous big red book in which Sinterklaas keeps a record of the children's performance. Pete lets it be known that the saint keeps excellent track of his constituents! After all, this is precisely what Pete helps him do all year long back home in Spain.

Pete might also carry a handful of birch rods or switches. It is said he uses these to punish naughty children. Though no one has ever really seen him do so, the rumors continue to keep the children on their best behavior. Sometimes, as a warning, Pete leaves a rod or switch with the treats. Badly misbehaved children may receive no treats at all, only the rod or switch.

A third prop for Pete is a large sack brimming with goodies. He tosses cookies, fruits (oranges are a particular favorite), chocolates, or other sweets to onlooking children. Some say this big bag, though delightful when full, is also large enough when empty to hold a naughty child of any size who needs to spend a year in Spain with Sinterklaas. Although some youngsters might question whether anyone ever suffers this punishment, all are unwilling to risk finding out.

Pete enjoys engaging in foolery with the children. Often he will not only join them in singing and dancing but will lead them as a chorus. He is always available to introduce a willing youngster to the famed Sinterklaas or to tousle a nearby head of hair. Tots and teens alike delight in his tricks and silly actions. Consequently, wherever Pete is found, there will inevitably be a group of young people surrounding him. They are all attentive, eager for fun, and hoping for a handout of some sort.

One of the delicious delights Pete is sure to carry in his sack is *pepernoten*. These are small, round, hard cookies flavored with spices of the season: cinnamon, nutmeg, anise, and cloves. The tasty nuggets are a regular sweet treat at St. Nicholas time. Pete would think of traveling nowhere without an abundant supply. He might even appear in a newspaper or magazine ad early in the season with the recipe. Then any cook can bake up a batch at home.

Pepernoten
(spicy cookie balls)

2 cups all-purpose flour
½ tsp. baking powder
¼ tsp. cinnamon
¼ tsp. nutmeg
¼ tsp. ground anise seed
¼ tsp. ground cloves
1¼ cups dark brown sugar, firmly packed
2 large eggs
1 Tbsp. diced candied orange rind

1. Sift flour with baking powder and spices. Add remaining ingredients and combine until mixture forms a dough.
2. With floured hands, form the dough into about 60 ½-inch balls and place on greased cookie sheets. Bake at 350° for 15-20 minutes, or until they are light brown. Store in an airtight container.
Yield: 60 small cookies

Pete sometimes breaks away from his tomfoolery to personally introduce a devoted onlooker to the benevolent saint (above). At other times, Pete dispenses tempting candies and cookies, along with serious advice about the importance of proper behavior (left).

Women often portray the elfish Pete. Here, a coed carefully arranges her pleated collar before joining St. Nicholas.

Before St. Nicholas' arrival and during his stay, the towns and cities of The Netherlands dedicate their decorations to Sinterklaas. Merchants launch advertising campaigns and special sales for St. Nicholas presents. Loudspeakers fill shopping malls with St. Nicholas songs. Large towns like Amsterdam and The Hague have colored lights strung over the streets. These are suitable canopies for Sinterklaas paraders. Later, when Sinterklaas departs, Christmas shoppers also enjoy them.

Small, doll-like figures of Sinterklaas and Pete can be seen in many displays, stirring anticipation in strolling shoppers. In large Dutch department stores like De Bijenkorf, large, almost life-size Pete dolls may climb ropes in a typical Pete-like antic. They lead all the way up to the towering ceiling.

Along with the bakeries and confectioneries, the costume store bustles with business during this season. Between the arrival of Sinterklaas and St. Nicholas Eve, people shop for the vestments the saint wears and for Pete's gay outfit. In the interests of credibility, imitators for both these celebrities must dress appropriately at all times. Sinterklaas and Pete will pop up at supermarkets, department stores, schools, hospitals, parties, and even in homes the night of December 5. The costume shops, therefore, are well stocked with robes, capes, headdresses, and other apparel for rent.

Some actors even train at a special center to portray the good saint properly at private parties and similar functions. The center provides important advice on saintly conduct. Careful instruction on costuming shows how to fasten wigs and beards. Woe to the Sinterklaas who loses his beard at an inopportune moment!

Since Sinterklaas is most imposing with a craggy face and a deep, resonant voice, women rarely play his part. They do, however, frequently portray Pete because they are generally smaller than men. A strong contrast between the two figures gives the imagination a boost and further enlivens the festivities in which they collaborate.

The light-hearted traditions of the Sinterklaas celebration might make one wonder how such playfulness ever attached itself to a saint. Who is St. Nicholas and where did he come from?

Some believe that Nicholas lived in Asia Minor from the year A.D. 271 to approximately A.D. 342. When the young man's wealthy parents died in an epidemic, he traded his life of luxury for a life of doing good deeds. A gift giver from the start, he distributed all of his wealth to the poor, then devoted himself to prayer. Soon he became the bishop of Myra. With this appointment came the splendid robes that he still wears today. A nickname from this time linked him, even that early, with children, one of his favorite groups. Nicholas became known as the "Boy Bishop," and his long life of extraordinary deeds was just beginning.

St. Nicholas would eventually become the patron saint of children, sailors and fishers, merchants, the persecuted, the imprisoned, and the poor. Lawyers and chemists also adopted him as their patron. Eventually St. Nicholas went international. He became the patron saint of countless cities, including Amsterdam, and of whole nations, as with Greece and Russia. Sailors in the Aegean wished one another luck with the saying, "May St. Nicholas hold the tiller." To be sure, over the centuries he has accepted this post whenever called upon and with all the magic that legend can provide.

Though gift giving is a trait common enough among well wishers, only St. Nicholas places gifts in stockings and shoes. The idea, it seems, came upon him accidentally. An unfortunate man was so poor,

his three daughters planned to sell themselves as slaves for lack of the dowries required for them to marry. Nicholas dropped three bags of gold through their window one night, and the girls were saved. This is one way St. Nicholas earned the faith of hopeful children the world over. The fact that one of the bags landed in a stocking "hung by the fireplace" to dry also gave St. Nicholas his unique calling card.

There are many other legends about this kindly saint. He revived three boys that an evil innkeeper had murdered. He crumbled prison walls in answer to the prayers of the persecuted. He even persuaded sailors to give portions of the grain from their holds to feed the starving poor. Then he mysteriously refilled the holds.

The saint also calmed stormy seas and restored the lives of those killed in shipwrecks. A group of Italian sailors was able to repay the saint in part for these and other favors. Almost 750 years after St. Nicholas' death, Myra fell into the hands of the Mohammedans. The sailors daringly stole the saint's remains and took them to Bari, a seaport in southern Italy. There St. Nicholas was reinterred, and an impressive church erected. The town and the famous basilica became, and remain, the center of the saint's worship in Europe.

St. Nicholas seems, however, to be more at home in The Netherlands than in any other country. Perhaps his popularity grew because his protégés included children, sailors, and merchants—three important groups in The Netherlands. In the 12th and 13th centuries, the tiny nation became the site of no less than 23 St. Nicholas churches. Some of these still stand today. As early as the 14th century, choirboys of the churches were given the day off on December 6. They chose their own "boy bishop" to represent St. Nicholas and paraded through the streets begging for "bishop money." Half the funds went to the church and half to the boys to spend on sweets.

By the 17th century, there were countless Dutch folk songs and legends about the saint, and famous painters drew subjects from his legends. Sweets called *speculaas* and *taai-taai* were associated especially with St. Nicholas. We know Jan Steen enjoyed these because they appear in his famous *The Feast of Saint Nicholas*. Perhaps Rembrandt, Frans Hals, and Jan Vermeer enjoyed them, too.

Today, time has completely trimmed away St. Nicholas' religious significance for the Dutch. Story-telling has relocated his home to Spain and given him Pete as a companion. Still, there is hardly another nation in the world that commemorates his feast day so widely and with such enthusiasm. His memory simply delights the Dutch. His feast day brings forth glad hearts, good cheer, and the gayest celebration of the year.

As the festive St. Nicholas parade comes to an end, the weary but contented families return to their homes. Now the children are filled with the mystery of the ingenious St. Nicholas and his wily friend, Pete.

Where did they meet? Where will they live in the coming weeks? Once down the chimney, how does Pete climb up again, especially with a naughty child in his sack?

While parents try to answer these baffling questions, Sinterklaas himself has but a fleeting moment to contemplate the season ahead. It will be a busy one for him and Pete. The two are well aware of the work cut out for them. There are schools to visit each day and children to check up on each night. There are records to keep and shoes to fill with goodies. Meanwhile, the rest of the nation knows the fun has just begun. The best is yet to come!

The legends of St. Nicholas found a responsive audience in the seafaring Dutch, who over the centuries dedicated many churches to the saint, including St. Nicolaaskerk in Amsterdam.

With his parade over, Sinterklaas contemplates three more weeks of bustling activities: school visits, shoes filled with goodies, and surprises by the basketful for his youthful admirers.

Saint Nicholas Eve

Every Dutch child from age 2 to 92 eagerly awaits St. Nicholas Eve. Truly, The Netherlands becomes a nation of the young by the evening of December 5, and rightly so. For, compared to the ageless St. Nicholas, who is old?

This is the night when St. Nicholas formally visits all Dutch homes. The tradition of holding parties in his honor on this date stretches far back into the country's history. One could say that the most famous party happened on canvas when Jan Steen painted *The Feast of Saint Nicholas*. The work immortalized the celebration. The domestic mayhem the master portrayed in this and other works also gave rise to a favorite Dutch saying. Whenever disorder rules at home, the usually tidy Dutch say they have a household "like Jan Steen." The comparison is apt almost anywhere in The Netherlands on December 5. Wrappings from presents accumulate on the floor and refreshments find their way around the room.

Dutch children know that Sinterklaas brings many of the delicious sweets of this season. But the marvelous Dutch bakers never fail to lend a helping hand. The confectioners of The Netherlands rank among the finest in Europe. They ably serve the Dutch people, themselves perhaps the greatest lovers of sweets. No one is surprised when, in early November, irresistible St. Nicholas goodies begin to appear in bakery shop windows. And even home is no haven for stoics when household cooks, armed with beloved family recipes and sweet bundles from the grocery, set themselves at the oven.

Bakery displays always include a luscious collection. *Borstplaat* is one rich Sinterklaas treat. This hard, smooth fondant, or sugar candy, comes in many flavors, including vanilla, fruit, coffee, and chocolate. Generally it appears once a year especially for this occasion. Often prepared in heart-shaped molds, borstplaat also takes the form of squares, circles, or stars—all in various sizes and colors.

Jan Steen (1626-1679) immortalized St. Nicholas Eve in The Feast of Saint Nicholas (above). *Today, goodies continue to overflow in Dutch homes that festive night* (right).

One shopkeeper in The Hague, it is said, wisely offers shoppers a piece of borstplaat to eat while they select their purchases. Inevitably, they return home with at least some borstplaat among their parcels.

Almond-based confections are also immensely popular. *Banketletters* are flaky puff pastries filled with an almond paste and shaped into a letter, usually an initial. The letter *M* seems to be the most popular. Not only is it generally the heaviest, but it is also appropriate for all mothers. The Sinterklaas Eve party would be incomplete without a large pastry letter adorning the serving table.

Perhaps the outstanding feature of the holiday season, however, is the baker's display of the remarkable confection known as marzipan. This is a rich almond-paste candy that comes in many guises. Bakers try to please the eye as well as the taste buds with marzipan. They have become true artists in producing these Sinterklaas specialties.

Bakers have made marzipan since the 1400's. Until the early 1900's, however, it came only in simple shapes and was generally plain white. Today, the assortment of marzipan that fills confectioners' cases is staggering. Bakers present it in every imaginable shape and color.

The Dutch frequently special-order the marzipan goodies as Sinterklaas gifts for friends and relatives. Often the selections have humorous meanings. Perhaps a marzipan squash racket is appropriate for a cousin who loves to play the game but has not yet mastered it. A marzipan telephone might go to a teen-ager who spends too much time on the phone at home. Marzipan teeth are perfect for a dear aunt who is always having trouble with her false ones.

There are countless other marzipan items to be seen at the bakery. Dice and wooden shoes are ex-

Bakers in The Netherlands mold marzipan candies into delightful objects, including little Dutch girls in full costume.

Borstplaat
(fondants)

1 cup sugar
3 Tbsp. liquid (water, milk, half and half, or light cream)
1 tsp. butter
few drops of flavoring or extract
few drops of food coloring

1. In a small, heavy saucepan, mix the sugar and liquid. Heat slowly to a boil without stirring until the syrup registers 240° on a candy thermometer.
2. Remove from heat immediately and add the butter, flavoring, and food coloring.
3. Stir vigorously until mixture thickens. Either drop from a spoon onto waxed paper or pour into greased lids no more than 1/3-inch high. Cool to solidify.

Variations:
For *fruit-flavored borstplaat,* add fruit or flavoring and appropriate food coloring.

For *coffee-flavored borstplaat,* the 3 Tbsp. of liquid should consist of 1½ Tbsp. strong coffee and 1½ Tbsp. half and half or light cream.
For *chocolate-flavored borstplaat,* add 2 Tbsp. unsweetened cocoa powder to the sugar and use 3 Tbsp. half and half or light cream for the liquid. Stir to dissolve any lumps before heating.
Yield: 12 medium candies

Carrots, ducks, and money pots are among the staggering assortment of marzipan that fills confectioners' cases at Sinterklaas time.

amples, as are fruits, vegetables, and dairy products. These may be realistic looking, like rounds of cheese, or comical, like dancing carrots. There are also innumerable animals. Pigs are a common choice, perhaps a reminder of the perils to the waistline when one eats too much marzipan. Often a bakery will have a life-size marzipan piglet on display, from which optimists may buy a large slice to take home.

There are marzipan versions of prepared foods of all sorts. Hamburgers, hanging sausages, fried eggs, and bowls of pea soup are on display. So are famous people. Pete is a great favorite.

Speculaas are another traditional treat during the Sinterklaas season. These are crisp, spicy, brown-sugar cookies, somewhat like gingerbread. Speculaas come in many different shapes, including windmills, animals, people, hearts, and even St. Nicholas himself.

The term *speculaas* comes from the Latin word *speculum,* meaning "mirror." Bakers press the dough

Speculaas
(St. Nicholas cookies)

1 cup softened, unsalted butter
2 tsp. vanilla
1 cup white sugar
1¼ cups dark brown sugar, firmly packed
2 large, beaten eggs
3½ cups all-purpose flour
2 tsp. baking soda
2 tsp. cinnamon
1 tsp. nutmeg
1 tsp. ground cloves
½ tsp. ginger
½ tsp. ground anise seed
⅛ tsp. salt

1. Combine butter and vanilla with the white and brown sugars and beat until light and fluffy. Add beaten eggs and blend well.
2. Sift the flour and all remaining dry ingredients together and beat into butter mixture.
3. At this point you may do several things:
Form cookies by rolling small pieces of dough into balls and baking on a greased cookie sheet for 10–15 minutes in a 350° oven.

Or, divide the dough into 2 equal rolls about 2½-inches in diameter, wrap well, and chill for several hours or overnight. After chilling, either cut the rolls into ⅛-inch to ¼-inch slices, place on greased cookie sheets about ½-inch apart, or roll the cooled dough out to ⅛-inch to ¼-inch thickness and use cookie cutters.
4. Bake at 350° for 10–15 minutes.
Yield: about 60 small cookies

Crisp, spicy speculaas *cookies are a favorite treat sometimes molded into the shape of dolls.*

for these cookies into carved wooden boards or planks. Each plank has a series of the same carving or any number of different ones. When the baker turns the cookies out onto a cookie sheet, the carved pictures appear as mirror images—hence, the name.

Carving these wooden molds of fruitwood and nutwood was once a baker's art. It required much skill, since the depth of each carving had to be the same all over for a cookie to brown evenly. Today, many of the original, hand-carved molds are valuable antiques and have become collectors' items.

If a mold is unavailable, speculaas dough may be cut with a cookie cutter, rolled into cookie balls, or sliced into rounds or rectangles before baking. A more elaborate version calls for a filling of almond paste between two layers of speculaas dough. Cut into squares, these speculaas look somewhat like brownies.

Sometimes bakers mold speculaas into large figures of men or women called "lovers" or *speculaaspoppen,* speculaas "dolls." Decorations for these cookies include white icing and almond halves. Some bakers prefer to sprinkle the cookie sheet with halved or slivered almonds before turning the molded cookies onto it. Whatever form speculaas take, these spicy cookies are a delight not to be missed.

Another type of cookie called taai-taai also comes in "lovers" shapes, or *taaipopjes.* Although similar to speculaas, taai-taai cookies have a honey base. They are also thicker and chewier than the thin, crunchy speculaas. Taai-taai cookies come in human forms other than lovers and in animal shapes as well. The baker frequently sculpts one piece of dough at a time and finally assembles a true work of art. Taai-taai creations can be as long as 1 foot (30 centimeters) and often weigh as much as 1 pound (448 grams). Families eat them in several sittings, of course, so that everyone relishes the delectable flavor for days.

Large chocolate letters are also a specialty of the Sinterklaas season. Chocolate is a particular favorite among the Dutch, regardless of its shape or the time of year it appears. But the chocolate Sinterklaas initials are an exceptional treat. They are available in plain or luxuriously fancy varieties of either dark, white, or milk chocolate. Some are hand-decorated with swirls of light or dark chocolate frosting, occasionally speckled with nuts or other decorations. What a dilemma, selecting just the right chocolate letter for a special gift!

The Netherlands teems with other chocolate delights in these merry weeks. The sight of them fascinates children at shop windows. Wooden shoes filled with sweetmeats, small figures of Sinterklaas, and lit-

Bakers can sculpt chewy taai-taai *into human and animal shapes—even a tableau of Sinterklaas, his famous horse, and Pete.*

All kinds of chocolate tempt the Dutch each November. Dark, white, and milk chocolate, molded chocolate, and stuffed chocolate are displayed in shop windows.

The children's fascination with Sinterklaas and Pete make the pair favorite subjects for drawings done both at home and at school.

tle dolls in the likeness of Pete are just a few of the many items molded in all varieties of chocolate.

Along with the treats come small, hollow staffs resembling the crosier St. Nicholas carries with him. The staffs contain an assortment of chocolates and other candies. It seems nothing is missing in the way of sweets in The Netherlands when Sinterklaas is in town. Who could wish for more?

Perhaps the only two persons busier than the bakers at this time of year are the saint and his helper themselves. By night, they ride across the country's rooftops listening through chimneys. The information-gathering tour tells them which children deserve rewards for obedience. On several of these nights, youngsters place a shoe near the hearth, the kitchen stove, or almost any outlet giving access to where the two may alight. The shoes hold carrots, some hay, or other snacks for the saint's horse. Perhaps a dish of water will stand nearby, as well, to quench the weary steed's thirst.

Pete, not Sinterklaas, descends the chimney or works his way through the gas pipes to pick up the horse's snacks and leave goodies for the young hopefuls. It would be a shame, after all, for Sinterklaas to soil his lovely robes. Pete also is the more agile of the two and always enjoys a good stretch and a stiff climb.

There is no home to which Sinterklaas and Pete will come every night. They have too much ground to cover in three weeks to visit everyone each day. Also, parents intervene. Father and mother are likely to remind their children, in the interests of Sinterklaas' budget, that they must not be overly demanding. And sometimes, when the children do put out their shoes, there will be no gifts left in the morning. This is a reminder that reason rules the day, even at Sinterklaas time.

In the past, Dutch children left wooden shoes by the hearth. Today, the custom has changed. Contemporary footwear has replaced wooden shoes both in everyday life and for St. Nicholas' visits. One custom is unchanging. Children who still "have their belief" stand a nocturnal watch behind couches, chairs, or any other makeshift fortification. From here they hope to sneak a peak at Pete when he arrives in the darkness. The trick never seems to work. But no generation has become discouraged enough to give up the vigil whenever they can remain undetected— they think—by their parents.

One method to entice Sinterklaas and Pete to the rooftop is singing. In the evening before going to bed, the children stand at the chimney and call to the saint with this favorite song:

Nicholas, I beg of you,
Drop into my little shoe,
Something sweet or sweeter,
Thank you, Saint and Peter.

In the morning, lucky children may find that their offering is gone. Some candy, a piece of fruit, or a small gift has taken its place. Often a note is there, as well, thanking the children for their thoughtfulness. It may also ask what they would like Sinterklaas to bring on December 5, when he makes his big visit with the best gifts. The youngsters, in turn, may respond the next evening with letters to the saint. The children often enclose a list of the items that they would most like him to bring on the big night.

Children's desires seem to be similar throughout much of the world. In The Netherlands, as in many countries, some of the gifts children request reflect current fads. Remote-control toys and dress-up dolls are always popular items, as are cars, trucks, trains, and games.

Goodies that the children might find before St. Nicholas Eve include pink and white candy hearts with creamy fillings, a taai-taai or speculaas doll, a chocolate figure, some marzipan, and an orange or tangerine. Small gifts such as a yoyo, a pad of paper, or a package of pencils are common. There will also be pepernoten scattered over the hearth. Any of these might also appear on St. Nicholas Eve.

Anything the saint leaves delights the children. In the morning they sing thank-you songs up the chimney in hopes for another visit soon.

Youngsters spend a portion of their time at home and at school drawing pictures of the friendly bishop and his jolly helper. This activity provides yet another device for winning the saint's favor. Sometimes delightful and always endearing, the illustrations go near the fireplace. The children hope that the pictures will please Sinterklaas enough to persuade him to leave an extra reward.

Sinterklaas and Pete never preoccupy themselves only with nightly home visits. By day, they appear with gifts and treats at orphanages, hospitals, and homes for the aged. The pair often visits supermarkets and toy departments at local department stores, as well. There, Pete keeps a weather eye out for fun-loving adults who might drop their composure for a moment to join him in jest.

Of the sweets Sinterklaas and Pete distribute to the youngsters, speculaas are the favorite handout. Pete's pepernoten run a close second. Since they lack the richness of so many other holiday sweets, they are popular for nibbling. Their small size and hardness also make them easy to transport and almost impossible to break.

Many problems tax Sinterklaas wherever he goes but rarely through any fault of the children. They are quite cooperative when meeting their generous friend. The real culprits are the parents, who sometimes prod bashful offspring into performing a song or dance, much to the children's embarrassment. Parents also may complicate matters by slyly slipping Sinterklaas notes about specific incidents of misbehavior from the past year. They expect the saint to translate the complaints into gentle yet effective reprimands. He somehow always manages to improvise. He remains fair, loving, and tolerant with the children, as well as diplomatic and patient with their demanding parents.

Sinterklaas relaxes with refreshments during his long appearances, but even these may provide problems. He especially enjoys lemonade or punch but may prefer to drink with a straw so as not to stain his beard. Hunger goes unsatisfied, and fatigue and sore feet are simply not allowed.

Schools are the most popular spot for personal visits from Sinterklaas and one or more "Petes." On arriving, they meet the children in the schoolyard. The students offer an exuberant welcome by singing a Sinterklaas song:

Good St. Nich'las is in Holland once again
With his horse and Peter from sunny Spain.
And even if he can't stay long,
We hope he'll stop to hear our song.
Dear St. Nicholas the door is open wide,
For you and Pete to step inside.
And we're singing, voices ringing, and our
  hearts rejoice
'Cause the saint loves all good girls and boys.

St. Nicholas is a good listener and greatly enjoys the entertainment the children provide.

From the schoolyard, the celebrants might proceed to the school gymnasium or to a large classroom. The children have been busy decorating and preparing the school for their illustrious visitors. Colorful paper chains might adorn the walls, doorways, and light fixtures. Children's drawings depicting the saint's arrival and the great parade will also appear. The children have enjoyed making masks or portraits of Pete, whose gay mode of dress makes him fun to draw. Now his likeness hangs in windows or on walls, further enlivening the schoolroom decor. A large, decorated chair will most likely provide an appropriate seat for the saint. Each child might wear a mitre made of red construction paper or a brightly colored paper beret complete with paper plume. How the class loves to imitate the saint and his jovial assistant!

Pete, of course, has his sackful of goodies and gifts ready to go. He tosses pepernoten in great handfuls all over the classroom. The children dive to the ground, vying to claim the treats. Pete loves the confusion and urges the children on.

Sinterklaas may find that Pete has gone too far in his mischief. He scolds Pete in front of the children and orders him to another part of the room. After all, Pete has to behave, too!

A little scolding never cools Pete's enthusiasm for fun. He supplies humorous antics for the children's benefit as long as he and Sinterklaas are with them. He is known to hop on chairs, tables, and shelves. The silly fellow has even poked wadded paper inside Sinterklaas' mitre—while it was still on the saint's head! Pete might also gleefully stuff a student volunteer into his sack: a warning to naughty children that Spain might be the best place for them this coming year.

The time arrives, however, to put all foolishness aside. A hush falls over the group as Sinterklaas opens his big red book. Pete stands nearby, a few birch rods in his hands. Gathered around the saint, the children listen carefully for their names. Does he know? Did he see? Of course, Sinterklaas knows everything! They are astonished at the truth his book holds. Could the teachers have supplied him with a few tidbits of information? No—Sinterklaas needs no help.

The good saint might have some children come forward to sing a song. He may also question them about their behavior. The young people show a wide

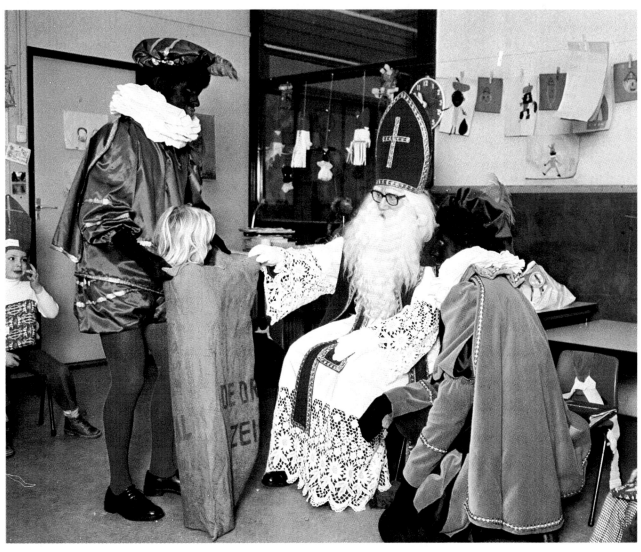

Serenading children greet St. Nicholas as he arrives in their schoolyard (left). A stout-hearted volunteer allows Sinterklaas' helpers to stuff her into Pete's sack, the same that carries naughty children back to Spain (below).

A hush falls over the classroom as Sinterklaas begins to read from his big red book.

range of emotions now. They may be brave, confident, apprehensive, shy, or even fearful at the sight of the overwhelming Sinterklaas. On some cheeks, an occasional tear of fright might glitter. This, however, quickly disappears at the comforting touch of an adult or through the twinkling smile of the loving bishop himself.

Sinterklaas almost always presents the schoolchildren with some sort of surprise from Pete's large sack. Perhaps they will each receive a small gift for fine behavior. Before departing, he promises to visit their homes with gifts if they, in turn, promise to be good. Who could possibly refuse?

Toward the end of November, the glowing feeling of cheerfulness and fun mounts throughout The Netherlands. St. Nicholas Eve is rapidly approaching. The final preparations for the important evening are under way. They always take up more time than ever expected.

The exchange of gifts among family and friends on December 5 is an incomparable event. The presents are never highly expensive or extravagant, nor are they beautifully wrapped. The tradition is, rather, to disguise or camouflage each present in an imaginative way. Its creative wrapping is a most important feature. Everyone calls the gifts "surprises."

A rhyme or poem always accompanies each surprise. Sometimes it expresses gratitude. More often, it humorously points out one of the recipient's quirks, foibles, or habits. Gentle teasing is this rhyme's goal. It is never meant to cause pain. The time is a special one, when good-natured kidding is not only expected but applauded. The camouflage and the verse, for example, might commemorate an incident or mishap of the past year. Although embarrassing at the time, it is now a source of joking. None other than Sinterklaas himself signs these surprises and verses, so that the giver remains anonymous. In some areas, Pete signs his name, too.

The clandestine activities of St. Nicholas Eve have given rise to the Dutch saying that best describes The Netherlands at this time of year. The entire nation "goes mysterious." For weeks, all have been shopping alone, secretly preparing surprises, and frantically writing verses in the isolation of dim corners of the house. Sometimes family members confine themselves to their rooms for long stretches. They even slam doors in faces, then stuff cotton in their ears while trying to compose clever rhymes. At work, no one is astonished to see an otherwise dignified physician hunched over a custard pudding on a desk. It will conceal a special gift. The nurse may be struggling to secure a package in the hollow of a loaf of bread. Everyone knows home is no place for this delicate task.

For those who are nervous about writing their own poems, local department stores generally employ a professional rhymester called a *sneldichter*. Sometimes with the aid of a rhyming dictionary, these speed poets can dash off a jingle in no time, all typed and ready for presentation. Half the fun of the holiday for many, however, lies in drafting these jolly rhymes on their own, regardless of the poetic quality. The more imperfect the verse, the more to laugh about.

St. Nicholas Eve is an exciting and busy day. Sinterklaas and Pete are still popping up all over town as last-minute shoppers crowd the stores until closing. People clog the streets, attempting to get home from shopping in time to take care of final wrapping and make ready for the fun.

Sinterklaas treats a little visitor to a surprise, then astonishes her with information about her behavior.

Department store rhymesters help customers prepare poems for surprise gifts (below). *Pete pops up on an antique bicycle to encourage a little one to sing for St. Nicholas* (right).

Most Dutch people must go to work or school on St. Nicholas Eve. Students would naturally struggle to remain attentive to studies on this last day for impressing the saint. But wise teachers usually devote the morning to class singing, opening surprises, or just plain merrymaking.

An exchange of gifts between older students often occurs grab-bag style. An alternative is to draw names before December 5. Anonymous donors can then match the surprise and poem to the recipients. They open the packages and read the verses one by one, to the hilarity of the rest of the class. Marzipan is a popular and inexpensive gift that lends itself well to humorous comments about classmates. The best present of all comes at noon, when the teacher dismisses class for the day.

Working adults are the unlucky ones. They are free to leave their jobs only in the late afternoon. Then they attend to last-minute details and hurry home to join in the festivities.

The vigil of St. Nicholas is traditionally a time for family gatherings. The party itself is warm and merry, with parents and children sharing the fun.

Many who find themselves away from the homeland suffer more nostalgia on this night than at any other time of the year.

After supper, Dutch children begin listening for the tapping of St. Nicholas' horse on the roof. They may sing a song to help speed his arrival or pass the time trying to remember what they asked for on their lists to St. Nicholas. Someone, maybe Papa, remembers that he left something at the office. He rushes off, promising to be right back.

Everyone jumps when a loud knock comes at the door or a sharp tap sounds at the window. Mama opens the door a wee bit. There is Pete's hand! It showers fistfuls of candies and pepernoten in the hallway. This rain of goodies on St. Nicholas Eve night has given it a special name: *strooiavond,* or "scattering evening."

The children fling themselves on the goodies, and then Pete is gone into the night. He has never shown his face. Only a bulging sack or basket of gifts remains on the doorstep.

There is a rumor that neighbors generally depend on one another for these mysterious deliveries. But there are no doubters in the homes where Sinterklaas and Pete make personal appearances. The good bishop sits down in Papa's chair—Papa is still missing—opens his big book, and kindly lectures each child at his feet about less than admirable traits. Sinterklaas may call the children one by one, saying, "Hans, you must learn to finish your dinner more quickly." Or, "Katrina, it is not nice to be cruel to the cat." Or, "It doesn't matter, Hilda, if you lose a game now and then." The children wonder, as usual, how he knows so much about them. None, however, would venture close enough to see whose handwriting is in the book, not even if they were calm enough to suspect their parents. Before departing, the saint may present each child with a gift. The youngsters know there are more to come.

There are two ways Sinterklaas goes about giving the children the rest of their gifts this night. They may put their shoes near the chimney again, sing St. Nicholas songs, and go to bed. Then St. Nicholas and Pete drop the presents through the chimney into the shoes, as on previous nights.

Elsewhere, Sinterklaas has already deposited the gifts somewhere in the house. The presents the saint gives the children right before he leaves may even have directions on where to find the rest of them. If this is the case, the children head for the treasure spots.

Another twist in Sinterklaas' strategy may provide for a large table somewhere in the house to be laden with the gifts for the children. Then they all search for the table together.

When the children become older, their surprises join those of the grownups in a heap on the floor. The pile of packages is the source of a second name for St. Nicholas Eve night. The Dutch call it *pakjesavond,* or "parcel evening." Each parcel carries the name of the person to whom it should go.

The Dutch are said to be masters at surprise giving. Their clever imaginations never seem to run dry. Neither does their enthusiasm for creations other than their own. This must be why they love Sinterklaas so much. He made up all the surprises tonight. Look! He has signed every one.

The family takes turns unwrapping the surprises and reading the poems. All listen intently and relish the jokes. Teen-agers in particular beam with pleas-

With St. Nicholas Eve at hand, parents hurry to finish surprise gifts for the family.

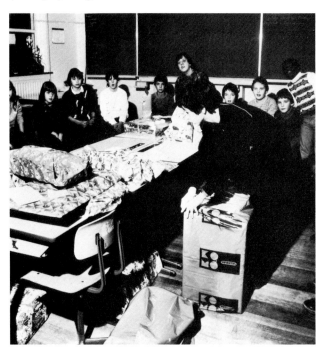

Teenagers open their school surprises one by one the morning of Dec. 5, wondering if they will ever learn the identity of the giver.

ure at some of Sinterklaas' cleverer tricks. His originality abounds.

A surprise, for example, may lie in a sausage, in a glove filled with wet sand, or in a gelatin loaded with fruit. A bracelet may come in a raw potato dressed up like a doll. But the possibilities continue. The potato could also be wrapped in tape, put into a milk carton, and placed in a bucket of ice along with a glass of cool refreshment. "Thank you, Sinterklaas!" Mother says aloud, toasting with the official tribute to the saint. It will be raised many times before the night is out.

Often tiny items like pocketknives lurk in immense receptacles like a rolled beef roast. On careful inspection, the roast turns out to be cotton well-basted with burnt sugar. A cast filled with plaster could go to someone who recently broke a leg. Imbedded in the plaster is a miniature pair of skates. A big bowl of porridge may go to someone who hates this food. He must eat the whole bowl in order to reach the surprise, which lies at the bottom.

Detailed treasure maps lead many on quests all over the house and even into the yard in order to find their surprises. Potato bins and coal cellars are excellent holders, as are flower pots, mail boxes, and drain spouts—if the weather permits.

One family member might open a message with his or her surprise only to find a blank sheet of paper. After much puzzlement, a telltale fragrance leads to the discovery that Sinterklaas wrote the message in lemon juice. Holding the paper to a flame reveals the writing, which sends the searcher to the last—or next—hiding spot.

What fun it is, seeing how Sinterklaas' surprises work! The longer the discovery takes, the better job he has done. So sometimes he confuses everyone by putting the wrong name on a package. Mother opens it, only to find a small box with father's name. Father opens the box to find a note sending his oldest son out the front door. There, on the step, is a molded chocolate figure. Ten minutes later, when the son breaks off a piece of the candy to eat, what should appear but a note for his little sister. She follows directions, looks in the kitchen sink, and there is a storybook signed by the saint.

Sometimes the surprises—with all due respect to Sinterklaas—are just a plain hoax. Candies filled with mustard, crackers made of soap, cookies with toothpaste icing all may appear from time to time. But everyone enjoys the inventive disguises and the dauntless labors Sinterklaas found time for again this year.

Children dream in front of a shop window filled with toys Sinterklaas might bring (above). At home, old hands and newcomers to the St. Nicholas festivities collaborate while making lists of the gifts they especially want (left).

On St. Nicholas Eve, surprises may lurk in books (below top), *in boxes* (right), *or in the bedroom* (below bottom).

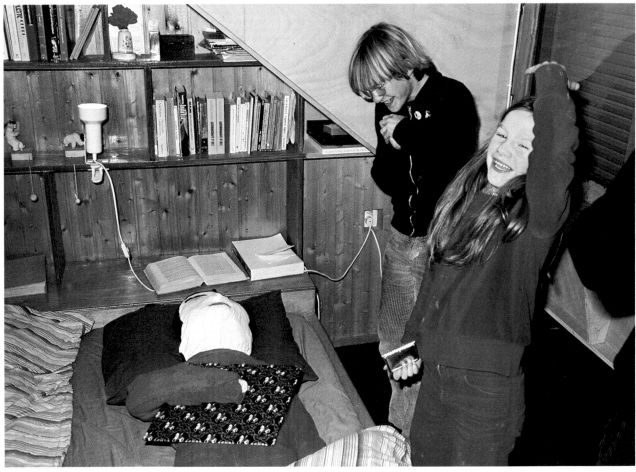

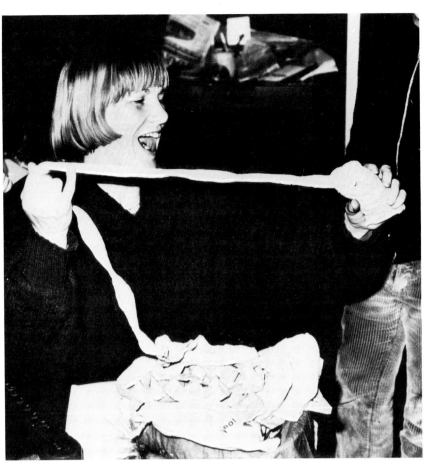

Unwrapping Mama's sticky surprise requires firm hands (left), *while Grandmother's treat appears only after delicate maneuvering* (below).

When all the surprises are finally open, the room is "like Jan Steen." Papers and poems lie strewn about, boxes and bags clutter the floor. Crumbs are everywhere. But, no matter—the fun and laughter are worth the cleanup.

Some Dutch people take gift giving into their own hands on this night. They place surprises on other families' doorsteps, ring the bell, and run away as fast as they can. Sinterklaas never minds. Everything is still from him anyway.

Something, in the meantime, is wrong off the northern coast. The women and children of Ameland have disappeared! And so have the men. By dusk, all that is left are spooky invaders scouring the streets, brandishing clubs and blowing through buffalo horns that fill the silent landscape with an eerie din. Once again, Ameland, the "island of demons," is earning its name. The *baenfeijers* are taking over.

These ghostly "street sweepers" are really the men in disguise. All 18 years and older, they are participating in a rite that is associated today with Sinterklaas but whose origins are lost in the area's pagan past. Their mission is twofold. They want to conceal their identity and sweep the streets clean of all the women—who, with the children, have taken refuge at home for the time being. Any unfortunate female who ventures outside is due for punishment. A baenfeijer will chase her, waving his club. She will finally have to jump over the club in a show of submission. When the streets are finally empty, the baenfeijers, who are really advance troops, disappear. They are making way for another flood of invaders.

The children, though cooped up for a time, have no reason to complain. Their huge festival for the season already took place on December 4. They wait with the others for the buffalo horns to bellow again. Now the *Omes* are on their way.

Also called *Sundeklazen* here, these are the men once again, in a complete change of costume. For weeks they have devised the ingenious, carnival-like dress. Restrictions lessen now, and the women and children are free to go outside—with an escort. They may visit one of the many open houses or inns, where the Omes flit about, speak mysteriously through their buffalo horns, and insist that women and girls dance with them. They may pound on the floor with their clubs to summon their chosen partners. Those watching try to guess the identity of the masked merrymakers, for the Omes change their costumes each year. Sometimes they even wear more than one costume a night.

Dressed in weird costumes and armed with buffalo horns, the men of the Frisian Islands take over their towns—only until midnight—each Dec. 5.

With a hot cup of bishop's wine, revelers will raise a toast to Sinterklaas, Pete, and the merry close of another mirthful holiday.

Ameland is not the only place that is entertaining "guests" this evening. So are three neighboring islands. Vlieland suffers an invasion of *Sunderklazen,* Terschelling of *Sundrams,* and Schiermonnikoog of *Klozems.* These are the local counterparts for Omes. Their missions are similar.

The villagers of each island dance and enjoy the revelry until midnight. In some places, the masks are cast aside when the clock strikes 12. The village of Hollum in Ameland, however, preserves this celebration in its purest form. Here, the Omes vanish into the darkness from which they came. They never reveal their identity, but some say, they leave the women in charge again for another year.

In the rest of The Netherlands, families are beginning to relax. The children enjoy some sweets and one more drink of hot chocolate before going to bed, weary from the day's excitement.

The adults have their pastries and coffee, or perhaps some steamy *bisschopswijn,* or "bishop's wine." This delicious hot spiced wine tops off the evening perfectly. The children are now dreaming of Sinterklaas, their beloved saint. He is on his way to a well-deserved rest in sunny Spain.

Bisschopswijn
(bishop's wine)

1 orange
15 cloves
1 cinnamon stick
½ apple
½ cup sugar
2 standard bottles (2 fifths) claret
   (also called red Bordeaux wine)
apple juice (optional)

1. Stud orange evenly with cloves. Place in pot with other ingredients and simmer slowly at least ½ hour. Do not boil. To lighten beverage, add apple juice to taste while simmering.
2. Remove fruit and cinnamon just before serving. Ladle hot beverage into heat-proof cups.

Signs of Christmas

Christmas comes by small, quiet steps to The Netherlands. As the gaiety, fun, and surprises of Sinterklaas disappear into the past, serenity takes their place. The Dutch prepare to welcome Christmas reverently, celebrating the holy holiday in a meaningful, religious way. There are no gay parties now. Rather, a spirit of peace, good will, and family togetherness dominates the waning days of December. Christmas in The Netherlands is "happy" more than "merry." There is no hectic rush in the streets, no hustle and bustle.

This is not to say that signs of Christmas are absent in the business districts and byways of the . nation. To be sure, a great deal of activity, though quiet, blossoms throughout the country.

Most towns have a majestic Christmas tree that stands, beautifully lighted, in the main square or market place. Amsterdam's tree is before the Royal Palace in Dam Square. To the north, in Groningen, a tall, dark green pine may tower over the Grote Markt. The golden lights glitter like stars. These trees and many others are likely from Norway, a treasure house of some of the biggest and most beau-

tiful evergreens in Europe. The Dutch also count on Sweden and Finland for a great share of the Yuletide greenery that will adorn the flat landscape of The Netherlands.

The cities and towns sparkle with white lights strung high above the streets. Splashes of red and green cast a hazy glow from shop windows on misty evenings. Stores in large cities display bright decorations with small Christmas trees, boughs of holly, and greenery in lush clusters.

Large department stores wear traditional decorations of the season. Red and white paper bells, silver and gold garlands, and boughs of evergreen

Hendrick van Avercamp (1585–1663) captured Dutch good will and togetherness at Christmastime in Winter Scene with Skaters near a Castle *(above).* Today, giant Christmas trees in city plazas add to the serenity of the season *(right).*

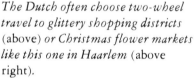
The Dutch often choose two-wheel travel to glittery shopping districts (above) *or Christmas flower markets like this one in Haarlem* (above right).

elegantly hang above busy shoppers at counters of lovely merchandise. Many departments have a Christmas tree gaily trimmed with white lights and colored ornaments. Santa Claus decorations may be present in some places, showing the growing influence of the famous character on the Dutch Christmas season. Colorful displays of Christmas and New Year's cards in Dutch and English are for sale in almost all department stores and stationers' shops.

Table decorations for the Christmas feast and decor for elsewhere in the home are an important part of the Dutch holiday that requires careful planning. Bicycles, a common means of transportation for the Dutch, stand abandoned outside stores. The owners shop, captivated by the amazing assortment of Christmas adornments.

Flower markets have a magnificent selection from which to choose. Open stalls fill with buyers purchasing fresh flowers, greenery, and garnishes for decorating. There are evergreen wreaths, holly branches, and an occasional sprig of mistletoe. Greenery comes bunched in baskets or is already grouped with fresh flowers and trimmed with a bow to make a festive wreath or centerpiece. Pine cones are loose or in pine-cone wreaths.

Bulb flowers like tulips and lilies are especially popular. Stalks of pussy willows will provide attractive accents at home. Red and white poinsettia plants are also popular among the Dutch, who often call them Christmas roses. Lovely candle arrangements ringed with evergreens and fresh flowers catch everyone's attention.

A wide variety of exhibitions takes place throughout the country at this time of year. Schoolchildren have a holiday of several weeks at Christmastime, so the family often enjoys these together when parents are also free. Kerstflora, for example, is a Christmas exhibition of bulb flowers that is held annually around the last week in December. Hillegom in the province of South Holland hosts the show. Here, familiar flowers as well as some unusual varieties bloom in a myriad of colors. The Christmas Market usually takes place during Christmas week in Rotterdam. This is a gift mart and fun fair that all enjoy.

Devotion and constant care result in the rainbow colors of Kerstflora, a magnificent flower exhibition held in Hillegom each Christmas.

Music is an essential part of the Yuletide season in The Netherlands. The Dutch love to sing and listen to music of all types, and Christmas only whets the appetite for more. Chimes and carillons sound over and over. Christmas melodies piped in at outdoor shopping centers echo as if from the heavens.

The Hague's Oudekerk, "Old Church," provides carillon concerts throughout the year. December finds entranced audiences enjoying them almost every afternoon. At the same time, many other churches and concert halls across the country offer musical performances. The variety would fulfill any preference.

Families that love ice skating will purchase tickets for "Holiday on Ice." This annual ice revue takes place each mid-December in The Hague. Costumed skaters present beautifully staged performances to a variety of music.

The wonderful fragrance of fir and pine wafting from Christmas tree stands tempts buyers to examine the choices. In Amsterdam, the sale always takes place on the Singel Canal. In the center of the old town, it is the city's innermost waterway. Beginning in mid-December, the bordering area closes off to traffic. Vendors unload all sizes of evergreens from flat-bottomed barges lined up along the water's edge. Holly branches and boughs and wreaths of fir and pine join the floating green display.

People drive, wheel, and walk to select their tree. Many a perfect choice has traveled home atop a small

Ornaments lure family shoppers to display cases in Amsterdam (right), *while trees arrive on barges in the old town's Singel Canal* (below).

School holidays leave children with plenty of free time to help Mama make homemade Christmas decorations.

sports car, astride a bicycle, or across someone's shoulders. The means of transport, of course, depends on the size of the purchase.

Trimming the Christmas tree is an activity for the whole family in The Netherlands, from selecting ready-made decorations to creating them by hand. The large department stores in most major cities have special Christmas decoration markets. Children and adults enjoy browsing among the brilliantly colored tree bulbs, sparkling tinsel garlands, and other gleaming decorations on display. The family will perhaps choose some new items for this year's tree.

A widespread custom, especially among apartment dwellers, is to purchase a yellowish paper star riddled with small holes through which the light from an electric bulb gleams. These three-dimensional decorations, called advent stars, shine in windows from early December. Their presence marks the time until Christmas. Perched in the windows of high-rise buildings, advent stars reflect a fiery checkerboard of Christmas cheer.

Families with single homes sometimes decorate their garden trees and front doors with lights. More common are frosty window-stars that families in all types of dwellings make with cutout star patterns and a can of artificial snow.

Ornaments that Dutch families make at home include small pinwheels made of colored foil and larger ones to adorn the treetop. Gilded, silvery, and many-colored walnuts may hang from the tree by virtue of thin wires secured within the nutshells. Bead garlands are easy to make and drape over the tree boughs. Fruits such as apples, oranges, and tangerines, though heavy, will also stay in their places with a little maneuvering and some string or wire. Pine cones are a versatile material with which the entire family may work—painting, glittering, and posing in the perfect spot.

Many decorations are possible to make with construction paper, wrapping paper, and a little glue.

Little hands are encouraged to help when the family trims the tree. As treats, ornaments may include tasty wreath cookies and chocolates of all shapes.

Besides ornaments, paper decorations include stand-up Christmas trees for the table or mantle and cutout designs for hanging in the window or on walls. Festive, hand-crafted placemats liven up the decor for children's Christmas parties.

The bakery also provides popular ornaments for the Dutch, who especially like to place edible decorations on their trees. How long these last, of course, depends on the children's appetites. Sugar bells and stars are favorites, as are various shapes of chocolates in foil wrappings. *Kerstkransjes* are small Christmas wreath cookies that are also easy to make at home. The family ties them to the tree with red ribbons.

Small candles are the last ornament to go on the

Sneeuwballen
(snowballs)

½ cup water
¼ cup unsalted butter
⅛ tsp. salt
¼ tsp. sugar
½ cup all-purpose flour
2 large eggs
2 Tbsp. dried currants or raisins
2 Tbsp. diced candied fruits or peels
oil for deep frying

1. Combine water, butter, salt, and sugar in a small, deep saucepan and bring to a boil. Boil gently until all the ingredients have melted. Remove from the heat. Add the flour all at once and mix rapidly with a wooden spoon to a smooth paste.
2. Add eggs one at a time, beating thoroughly after each addition. Add currants or raisins and candied fruits.
3. Heat oil to 375° and, with a metal spoon that should be dipped in the hot oil, drop the dough by spoonfuls into the oil. Fry 5–8 minutes, or until puffed up and golden brown.
4. Drain on paper towels and dust with powdered sugar.

Yield: 8 large or 16 small snowballs

Fresh garlands and fragrant candles bring the season's spirit to a quiet corner of the house (left). *Chilled from shopping, a family hurries home to enjoy some hot chocolate and sugary "snowballs"* (below).

tree. Many Dutch families use only red or white candles in silver holders. Once lighted, this decoration demands a perpetual guardian. Perhaps a bucket of water and a stick with a rag will also be ready nearby in case of emergency. When the rest of the room is darkened, the final effect of the illumined candles is an enchanting glow. It reflects the warmth and light of the true meaning of Christmas.

By Christmas Eve, larger candles glow from the dining table, side tables, the mantle—almost anywhere. Garlands of evergreen branches, embellished with pine cones and even fruits and vegetables, might frame windows and doorways. Together, the fragrant candles and sweet-smelling boughs fill the house with quiet pleasure.

In Catholic homes, there will probably be a *kerststal,* or crèche, near the Christmas tree. The children in these families enjoy setting the figures of the Nativity in just the proper arrangement. The crèches also appear in Catholic churches and chapels.

After a family shopping trip in the brisk December weather, the family may settle down before the Christmas tree. The children enjoy some hot chocolate and a warm batch of delicious *sneeuwballen.* These "snowballs" are deep-fried spoonfuls of cream puff dough dotted with candied fruit and currants or raisins. A good dusting of powdered sugar on top resembles snow. A special delight during the entire month of December, sneeuwballen are also a treat for New Year's Eve.

Anytime during the Christmas season, Dutch families enjoy Christmas stories. Reading aloud by the light of the Christmas tree is a time-honored custom. A favorite legend is that of "The Three Skaters":

The canals stretched straight and frozen till they faded away in the distance. Gnarled old willows stood in ragged rows like worried onlookers. The year's harvest had been poor. Farmers wondered how they would manage to pull through the winter.

One farmer skated home over the frozen canal. He had been to market that day. All he was able to get for his few pennies was a bagful of apples, now slung over his shoulder. He hurried along, thinking how disappointed the family would be with the meager results of his marketing, and Christmas so near.

Then through the falling dusk appeared his neighbor, a miller. He carried a few loaves of bread the baker had given him in exchange for a sack of flour. The two skaters greeted each other without a word as they traveled on through the silent evening. Each sank into his own thoughts, knowing that the other man's were the same.

Soon another neighbor joined them, this time a pig farmer. He carried a side of bacon for which he had found no buyer in town.

The strong, regular strokes of the silent men's skates were the only sounds in the wide, wintry landscape. It was getting even colder now. The men huddled deeper into their woolen mufflers.

The heavy clouds began to look strangely lit, as by an inner light. The skaters noticed the moon appearing from behind the clouds. One cold, stark beam pointed straight down to a decrepit, lonely barn across the snow-covered pasture on the left.

Suddenly a sound came from the barn, the sound of a baby crying. "Hey!" the miller called to his companions. "Hey, there, stop!" The other two halted, annoyed with him. It was cold and late—time to be home.

"Listen!" said the miller, pointing his finger to the barn. There was no mistake. The others heard it, too. There was a baby crying there.

"But that barn's been empty for years," said the farmer.

"An old man keeps his sheep there," added the pig farmer, "but that's no bleating."

For a moment the three men hesitated. Then they removed their skates and crossed the pasture to investigate. As they approached the moonlit barn, the crying became quieter as a woman's gentle voice began to hum a soft lullaby. The neighbors were baffled. Then the miller moved forward and opened the door. Their eyes adjusted to the dim glow of the lantern inside. They saw that their ears had not deceived them.

A young woman they had never seen before sat on the cold floor. In her arms she held a newborn baby. Her coat was wrapped around the little boy, who was now sleeping peacefully. An old man was raking together some hay in a corner. Now the mother laid down her baby tenderly on that little heap of softness in the cold, rough barn.

"We come from far away," the old man began to explain, as if to answer unspoken questions, "and we still have far to go. It was time for the wife to have the baby. We are grateful that we found this barn. But we can't stay long, for we have no food and no firewood. We shall have to move on tomorrow."

The three men just stood for a moment, unable to speak. Then, driven as by one force, each lowered the sack from his shoulder and emptied it in front of the young mother. The apples, the bread, and the bacon gleamed curiously in the flickering lantern light. Her eyes shone with peace and quiet acceptance. They felt a sense of well-being so strong that they were puzzled. One by one they took a shy look at the dozing infant, gathered their empty sacks, and turned to leave. Gently they closed the door behind them.

Back at the canal, they tied on their skates, swung the sacks over their shoulders, and started on the last stretch home. They all wondered about the little scene they had just taken part in. Strangely, none was worried about coming home empty-handed. They felt almost light-hearted in the cold, frosty night.

The sacks they carried soon seemed to be getting heavy. By the time they reached the village, the three skaters almost bent double under the load. Why, they could not explain.

At the church, the three men parted. The last few steps home seemed almost unbearable, so heavy was the weight on their shoulders. They opened their back doors and stepped inside. They dumped the sacks on the floor and looked at the expectant faces around the fireplace.

"Father is home!" The youngsters jumped up and began to tug at the sacks. They pushed, laughed, and

The forlorn peace of a wide, wintry landscape sets the mood for a favorite Christmas story, "The Three Skaters."

romped, as if they had discovered a new kind of game.

When the men finally opened the sacks and turned them out over the kitchen floors, food of all sorts rolled across the neatly scrubbed tiles. There was candy for the children, Dutch honey cake for the mothers, and fruits for the fathers. What happy feasts they had that evening in all three homes!

When there was quiet again, the three men sat contentedly, each at his fireplace. But in spirit they were far away. Their thoughts hovered around a moonlit barn, around a simple, lanternlit scene, where a miracle had come to pass.

The Christmas story ends and bedtime is near. The children of The Netherlands help blow out the candles on their Christmas tree one by one, marking the end of another evening. Kerstmis, the tranquil Christmas celebration, is one day closer.

Christmas One and Two

Christmas Day comes not once but twice a year for families in The Netherlands. December 25 is First Christmas Day. Second Christmas Day follows on December 26. Although the Dutch observe these two holidays somewhat differently, they devote both to faith and family.

There is, of course, only one Christmas Eve, and it is a workday. Some people may be off work in the afternoon, providing extra time to stock up on groceries for the Christmas feast tomorrow. Some will take the opportunity to visit with relatives. In the evening, many families attend church services, beginning the strict religious observance that characterizes First Christmas Day.

Christmas Morning finds other families going to worship. They wish one another *"Vrolijk Kerst-feest,"* "Merry Christmas," as they meet. Most churches greet their congregations with Christmas trees and elegantly decorated altars. Evergreens and fresh flowers make the special services even more beautiful. So do the inspiring voices of the choirs.

Hearts are filled with good will and thanksgiving as families return home for *koffietafel* late Christmas Morning. This meal is not breakfast, which took place before the trip to church. It is, rather, an elaborate version of breakfast served as lunch. The meal is called "coffee table" because coffee is generally served.

Today, koffietafel will probably feature *kerstkrans*. This is the same banketletter pastry served at St. Nicholas time. Today it has turned into a large Christmas wreath decorated with lemon icing, candied fruit, holly, and a big red bow. The kerstkrans is heavy and rich and quite suitable for serving as a dessert for those who would rather avoid sweets at lunch.

In some areas of The Netherlands, such as the large cities in the west, the exchange of gifts is

Pieter Bruegel the Elder (1525?-1569) expressed the quiet reverence of Christmas in The Netherlands in The Counting at Bethlehem *(above). A choral concert Christmas Morning inspires worshipers at The Hague's Grote Kerk (right).*

Happy is the holiday when a hard frost sets in and skaters can take to the ice on beautiful frozen lakes and canals in The Netherlands.

becoming popular and may take place this morning. The presents, however, are modest in nature and totally without the diversion of the "surprises" that St. Nicholas brings. A carefully chosen book makes an appropriate gift.

In the provincial villages of the east, this custom is uncommon. Solemn and conservative observances prevail. In the south, some people believe in Father Christmas, called de Kerstman. He may bring presents to families in this region, just as he brings them to families in Germany and Belgium.

Overall, however, the Dutch get their Christmas cheer from one another. The afternoon finds most homes welcoming relatives and close friends. People do puzzles and play quiet board games. Perhaps they listen to concerts, choral programs, and religious services aired on TV especially for First Christmas Day.

In the Frisian Islands, a family in traditional winter costume takes a pass through town in an antique sleigh drawn by a Frisian horse in Frisian harness (left). Crowded ice paths may require two-way traffic as a safeguard against collision (below).

There are also concerts to attend for those who prefer an outing, plus some school plays.

Families could have reservations to dine at a restaurant. More than likely, however, the kitchen is bustling with preparations for Christmas dinner.

During the course of the day, the family will sing and play Christmas songs with undwindling zeal around the tree. Favorite Dutch carols vary, but one that everyone knows is "Er Is een Kindeke Geboren," "A Little Child Is Born." Others include carols famous the world over, especially "Silent Night."

To stay their hunger until dinner, the Dutch may nibble on a delicious sweet Christmas bread called *kerstbrood*. Also found at Eastertide, this bread is riddled with raisins, currants, and candied fruit peel, then dusted with powdered sugar.

If the weather permits and a hard frost has set in, the entire family enjoys the favorite pastime of all Dutch people: ice skating. Even the cooks will leave the kitchen on First Christmas Day for a twirl on the ice. The beautiful frozen lakes and canals of The Netherlands are dotted with colorful skaters, almost like a scene from Bruegel or Avercamp.

Everyone in The Netherlands skates whenever possible, from grandparents to small children. Those youngsters just learning push a chair along the ice in front of them. Families stay together by each hooking an arm over a long pole as they skate. Grownups even push baby carriages along the ice. Antiques such as sleighs and baby carriages with runners frequently make an appearance at Christmas.

Kindergarten "angels" in Eemnes visit Mary and Joseph with a song of love and a dance of joy in a play about the First Christmas (right). Three generations come together Christmas Night to share a candlelit dinner (below).

The lovely windmills of The Netherlands provide a quaint backdrop for the playful melee. Of the 10,000 windmills once found here, about 1,000 remain, most dating from the 18th and 19th centuries. East of Rotterdam, the town of Kinderdijk has 17 windmills. Spotting the frozen landscape, they provide a picturesque backdrop for skating or taking a jaunty sleigh ride.

Seven o'clock is the traditional Christmas feast time. The meal is abundant, the atmosphere formal. Many Dutch families read from the Bible at the Christmas feast. According to custom, either the oldest or the youngest reader presents favorite passages that punctuate the reverent tenor of the day.

The candlelit table draped in white linen may have a white or red poinsettia centerpiece. Holly and other greenery furnish added decoration. Fresh irises or tulips, perhaps the gift of an appreciative guest, bring even more loveliness to the dinner table.

The menu varies from family to family. It might begin with appetizers such as *bitterballen,* or cocktail meatballs, and *zoute bolletjes,* "salted bullets." The bitterballen are small croquettes of finely minced veal or beef in an herb-laced gelatin. They take some time to prepare, but adults especially enjoy them with an apéritif of Genever, famous Dutch gin. The bullets are salty pastry dabs baked to a fine crunch.

A savory bowl of *groentensoep,* Dutch vegetable soup, follows, sometimes served with little fried meatballs. The fish course, *mossel-rijstschotel,* is a delicious, Indonesian-style casserole of mussels over cream-smothered rice. Indonesia, once a Dutch colony, has shown its influence on much of The Netherlands' cuisine.

Ham is a winter delight in The Netherlands. It could provide the entree for the Christmas meal in the form of *lof, ham en kaassaus.* Here, ham slices are wrapped around gently braised endive and crowned with a golden layer of sharp-cheese sauce. A steaming side dish of Dutch-style asparagus passed around the table with hard-boiled eggs and butter sauce complements the ham. Game in the form of roast hare, goose, and venison are popular fare. These as well as turkey often appear as the entree.

As the table is cleared and coffee served, everyone still has room for a light dessert. This year it is *bessensappudding,* a delicate, yet tart, currant pudding.

Diners relish cookies and chocolates next, along with more coffee. Chocolate bells and wreaths are common, plain or topped with chopped nuts or sugary sprinkles.

The Theater Zuidplein in Rotterdam delights Christmas audiences with the antics of the characters in Cinderella and the Three Musketeers.

Only candles light the buildings of Gouda's market square as the mayor turns on the town's dazzling tree in the annual Christmas ceremony called "Gouda by Candlelight."

Bessensappudding
(currant pudding)

4 eggs, separated
1 cup crushed currant juice and ½ cup brown, firmly packed sugar *or* substitute 1 cup frozen, concentrated cranberry cocktail juice, omitting all or part of the sugar
1 envelope unflavored gelatin, softened in ¼ cup water

1. Stir yolks (and sugar) till thick and foamy. Add juice and heat mixture on low flame until somewhat thickened and the foam has mostly disappeared.

2. Dissolve softened gelatin in this mixture. Fold in beaten egg whites and cool, stirring occasionally until egg whites and custard no longer separate.
3. Pour into pudding mold rinsed with egg white or oil. Chill and unmold. Serve topped with sweetened whipped cream and with wafers or ladyfingers. Yield: 6 servings

Ringing bells and the sweet voices of the choir bring the spirit of Christmas to families gathered around the glowing tree at Gouda.

December 26, Second Christmas Day, is as sedate and refined as December 25 but not so home centered. More people call on friends and dine out. They also attend performances of all sorts. Churches, concert halls, and auditoriums throughout the country present choral, instrumental, and theatrical performances, both amateur and professional.

Children, led by teachers and Sunday school instructors, take part in choirs and Christmas plays in schools and churches. The plays usually depict the Nativity story. Each child takes a part. Not a character is forgotten. The children play the Holy Family, the Three Kings, the shepherds and angels—even the donkey that carries Mary. A baby brother or sister might portray the Infant Jesus.

Almost every Dutch community has at least two amateur choral groups that perform on Second Christmas Day. Local brass bands or orchestras, ensembles, and professional vocalists provide audiences with an opportunity to listen yet another day to the inspiring carols of the season.

A popular, newly established presentation in Rotterdam is the Christmas Pantomime at the Theater Zuidplein. Not a pantomime in the strict sense, the play has a goal of audience participation. The subject of the play *Cinderella and the Three Musketeers,* for example, is a combination of a fairy-tale and folk tale. Current events are worked into the script, with songs and spectacle riveting everyone's attention to the stage. In this and other pantomimes, there is always a villain, a hero, and a sweet heroine. She always needs and asks for help from the children in the audience. Animated by the happy production, they always oblige.

One spectacular Christmas sight graces the little town of Gouda in the province of South Holland. It is a towering Christmas tree lighted in mid-December in the ceremony called "Gouda by Candlelight."

This pageant takes place in Gouda's market square in front of the beautiful Gothic Town Hall. The oldest in the country, the town hall dates from 1450. With a little imagination, those who attend the opening ceremony find themselves back in the 16th century. No electric lights glare in any of the buildings facing the square. Instead, all the windows surrounding the square and those of the town hall shine with the soft glow of candles. The mayor throws the switch illuminating the huge evergreen, which overwhelms the scene. Carillons peal and a choir sings forth. Everyone in the crowd joins in, even foreign visitors who do not speak Dutch. These people sing along in their native language, with the encouragement of their Dutch hosts.

Though Christmas Days come to an end for many families at the foot of Gouda's tree, the spirit of Christmas endures for whoever stood in the splendid glow. The lofty branches rise as a tribute to tradition, beauty, and fellowship for The Netherlands—and the world.

Twelve Days of Christmas

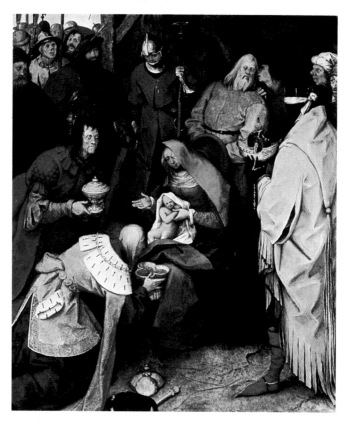

Holiday spirit in The Netherlands spills over into the Twelve Days of Christmas. With the glee of Sinterklaas and the joy of Christmas over, there are still two more special days to go: New Year's and Three Kings' Day. Two winter activities will also end in final contests. They are midwinter horn blowing and a bell-ringing custom called St. Thomasluiden.

Since the first Sunday of Advent, folk in the eastern, rural province of Overijssel have heard weird tones sounding nightly in the distance. These are the result of midwinter horn blowing, called *midwinterhoornblazen*. The Yuletide tradition's origins probably date back to approximately 2500 B.C. Once believed to drive away evil spirits, the sound of the horns still haunts the broad, frosty landscape.

The instruments have great carrying power. On cold, icy nights people can hear their monotone from over 3 miles (5 kilometers) away. The tones receive answers from farm to farm in a joint announcement of the coming of Christ.

Among others, the villages of Twente, Denenkamp, Oldenzaal, and Ootmarsum join in this ancient custom. The horn makers start months ahead. Summer will find them carving the horns by hand from the hollowed limbs of birch or elder trees. The task is formidable.

First the horn makers must find a tree of suitable size and shape. The trunk is then sawed, planed, chiseled, dried, hollowed, and bound. The result is a horn that is quite long and slightly curved. To be effective, the midwinter horn must be wind-tight as well as flawlessly constructed.

The strange sound that comes from the midwinter horns gets louder when the farmers play them above farmyard wells. The players must place and blow through the horns with an expertise won only through much practice.

Pieter Bruegel the Elder's The Adoration of the Kings *depicts the coming of the Magi to Bethlehem, an event the Dutch celebrate yearly as Three Kings' Day* (above). *Midwinter horns have probably sounded across Dutch farmlands since 2500* B.C. (right).

The bellhouses of Friesland ring out during the entire Twelve Days of Christmas. The custom, which has given rise to annual competitions, is said to scare away evil demons that lurk at year's end.

By the time people are sending their New Year's cards, final competitions in midwinter horn blowing are taking place. The champions will earn the respect of neighbors for the year. The winners often come together to perform unique compositions. These can usually be heard daily through January 6.

Another age-old tradition that appears to be a relic of pagan custom is St. Thomasluiden, or St. Thomas ringing. This practice of continuous bell ringing takes place only at the *klokkestoelen,* or bellhouses, in the cemeteries of Friesland.

The custom began in the southeastern portion of the province. It may have been yet another device for dispelling demons that lurked at year's end. Some link the tolling of the bells with the death of St. Thomas à Becket, venerated in Friesland as well as in England. Archbishop of Canterbury, he was murdered in his cathedral on December 29, 1170.

The difficult art of St. Thomas ringing consists of ringing two bells in harmony. One is large and heavy, the other small and light by comparison. Correctly rung, they produce a fascinating counterpoint.

St. Thomas ringing occurs today from December 21 through December 31. Young and old try their hand at tolling the bells. Anyone from 16 to 21 years may compete in the championships.

New Year's Eve, which the Dutch call "Old Year's Evening," arrives amid great excitement all over The

Netherlands. For the Dutch, this is a time for festive togetherness. They refer to December 31 and January 1 jointly as "Oude/Nieuw," or "Old/New." Most want to be with their families cheerfully to celebrate the events of the two days.

In the late afternoon, streets crowd with workers rushing home from shops and offices. To one another, they call out *"Zalig Uiteinde!"* meaning "Blessed End." The entire nation shuts down to celebrate the new year. Finding public transportation—even a taxi—available after 9 o'clock on New Year's Eve is almost impossible.

Many families attend church services early in the evening. Some will also have Bible readings at home. Then the evening gives way to games, charades and other amusements—and refreshments. As many generations of a family as possible attend. Even the young ones may stay up late to share the fun and welcome in the New Year.

A light supper is generally served around 11 o'clock. Usually it is a cold buffet with all sorts of delicacies and pastries for dessert. Three treats that are favorites this time of year use apples as a base.

Appelbollen are whole apples cored and then scrumptiously wrapped as buttery dumplings in puff pastry. With a cinnamon mixture inside, they are baked into golden balls. *Appelflappen* are batter-coated slices of apple that sizzle when taken from the

Oliebollen *by the bucketful are the New Year's treat these Spakenburg women prepare. Each doughy scoop of batter teems with chewy currants and chunks of crunchy apple.*

deep-fryer. The most popular and universal of all New Year's Eve refreshments is *oliebollen*. These crunchy doughnuts are loaded with currants and chunks of apple.

In the province of Limburg, merrymakers may bite into succulent wedges of *Limburgse vlaai*. A regional year-round favorite, the "Limburg pie" carries a healthy topping of fruit. In season, the fruit is baked fresh on the frothy dough. For New Year's, canned peaches or plums make good substitutes that all enjoy.

The hour before 12 midnight, the TV has the year's news wrap-ups. The family stays tuned until about 11:45. Then, swallowing the last morsels of

Appelflappen
(apple fritters)

Fritter batter:
1 cup all-purpose flour
½ tsp. salt
1 Tbsp. corn oil
½ cup water or milk
2 egg whites, stiffly beaten
oil for deep frying
powdered sugar

1. Sift flour and salt into a bowl. Make a well in the center and add oil and water or milk, beating until smooth. Allow to rest for 45 minutes to an hour.
2. Fold in the beaten egg whites with a rubber spatula.

Apples:
4 to 5 tart apples
1 cup light brown sugar, firmly packed
1 Tbsp. cinnamon
1 tsp. nutmeg

3. Peel and core apples and slice into ¼-inch to ½-inch rings.
4. Coat with sugar that has been mixed with the cinnamon and nutmeg.
5. Heat cooking oil to 375°. Dip coated apple slice into fritter batter and fry in hot oil. Turn several times until both sides are golden brown.
6. Drain on paper towels and sift with powdered sugar.
Yield: 4–6 servings

Groups from the Island of Marken don traditional costumes to enjoy winter holidays on the ice (above). In North Brabant, Three Kings' Day finds children in biblical guise waiting to begin a neighborhood parade for goodies (right).

their New Year's treats, the youngsters run outside to prepare the fireworks, which are legal only on New Year's.

The clock strikes 12 and boom! The noise begins. All factories in the town and all ships in the many harbors blast their whistles. Church bells peal and carillons play. Firecrackers explode on the ground and fireworks light up the sky.

Inside, there is a moment of thanksgiving. Then glasses clink and relatives embrace. They wish each other *"Een Gelukkig Nieuwjaar!"* or "Happy New Year!" Champagne, bishop's wine, or rum punch come from the head of the household, who offers his toast to the coming year. Then the festivities go outside again as neighbor visits neighbor to give good wishes for the New Year. The children finally go to bed, but most of the adults continue to celebrate into the wee hours.

New Year's Day is a legal holiday in The Netherlands. Most people sleep in late to recover from the long celebration the night before. The remainder of the day, people continue their visits to friends and relatives. Somehow, everyone manages to find room for all the traditional cakes, fruit loaves, and pastries, which come out in force again today.

Time was in The Netherlands when freezing winter temperatures during the Twelve Days of Christmas made the ice perfect for races and ice celebrations. Recent years have seen a warming trend, and towns and cities have had to cancel many of these. With luck, however, costumed groups still take celebrations to the frozen canals. Whole banquets have been served there on the Island of Marken, with dancing and free-skating to follow.

Wherever ice skating takes place, vendors likely sell warm foods and drinks. Skaters taking a breather hold steaming cups of *erwtensoep,* the Dutch pea soup also called *snert.* They may also purchase warm, anise-flavored milk as they hop from one canal to the next for skating.

January 6, the feast of the Epiphany, is known as Driekoningendag, or Three Kings' Day. The young are generally the focus of the activities on this day. An Epiphany cake with a bean cooked inside is the center of their attention. Sometimes this cake is a *tulband,* which is similar to Christmas bread, only baked in a bundt pan.

The cake is served to the youngsters. Whoever finds the bean in his or her piece of cake becomes monarch for the day. A gold paper crown sets the lucky one apart from the courtiers.

There is another Three Kings' Day custom in some parts of The Netherlands. It takes place especially in the predominantly Roman Catholic

Under the direction of vigilant fire-fighters, the Dutch commit another happy Christmas season to the past in the blazing glow of a Christmas-tree bonfire.

provinces of North Brabant and Limburg. The children dress as the Three Kings, as shepherds, or as angels. Then they parade through the streets of their neighborhoods carrying candles or homemade stars and Chinese lanterns. They sing Epiphany songs as they march along. Often, they will go from house to house, where they receive treats.

Three Kings' Day marks the official end of the winter holiday season in The Netherlands. On January 6, families take down all Christmas trees and decorations, if they have not done so already.

Many Dutch towns hold an organized burning of Christmas trees. Local firefighters are always on hand to keep the activities in order. The match is struck and the trees go up in a blaze, so ending another Christmas season for The Netherlands.

With the Christmas season comes an irresistible array of treats from Dutch bakeries and from the family kitchen. Featured above (from top to bottom) are an M-shaped banketletter ringed by assorted cookies, golden brown appelbollen, and a wedge of kerstbrood in its blanket of powdered sugar.

Dutch Treats

Appelbollen
(apple dumplings)

Shivering Dutch skaters went home to hot beverages and rich treats much like those served today when Frans Huys created this line engraving in the mid-1600's. Skaters Before the Gate of Saint George in Antwerp is after a picture by Renaissance master Pieter Bruegel the Elder (above).

Dough: As for *banketletters*, page 67.

Apples:
6 tart apples
½ cup light brown sugar, firmly packed
1½ tsp. cinnamon

1 egg, beaten

1. Peel and core apples. Mix brown sugar with cinnamon and fill each apple with about 2 Tbsp. of mixture.
2. Roll dough out to about ⅛-inch thickness. Cut the dough into squares large enough to enclose the apples.
3. Place apples topside down on each square of dough and wrap the dough around the apple, corner to corner. Moisten the dough edges with a little water to seal and then press edges together. Prepare each apple in the same way.
4. Arrange the dumplings, seam side down, in a buttered baking dish. Brush each one with a mixture of 1 egg beaten with 1 Tbsp. water.
5. Bake at 425° for 10 minutes and then 45 minutes more at 350°. Dumplings are done when the crust is golden brown and the apples are cooked through.
Yield: 6 apple dumplings

Kerstbrood
(Christmas bread)

2 packages dry yeast
¼ cup very warm water
¾ cup milk at room temperature or slightly warmed
½ cup sugar
½ tsp. salt
½ cup softened, unsalted butter
3 large, lightly beaten eggs, reserving 1 egg white
1 cup raisins or currants, or a mixture of both
½ cup diced citron
½ cup diced orange peel or candied fruit
4¼ cups all-purpose flour
¾ cup chopped, blanched almonds
2 tsp. cinnamon
½ cup powdered sugar for dusting

1. Mix the yeast with the water and stir to dissolve. Add the milk, sugar, salt, butter, and 2 whole eggs plus the yolk from the third egg. Blend well.
2. In a separate bowl, dust the raisins, currants, citron, and orange peel or candied fruit with a little of the flour and the cinnamon, and then add the almonds.
3. Add half the flour to the yeast mixture and stir until smooth. Cover and let rise in a warm place until doubled in bulk, about 1 hour. This mixture is called a sponge.
4. Add the remaining flour and knead until smooth and elastic, about 5 minutes. Knead in the fruits and nuts.
5. Place the dough in an oiled bowl, turning the dough so it is completely coated. Cover and let rise for about 30 minutes.
6. Divide the dough into 2 equal portions and press each dough ball into a large, flat circle. Fold each circle over so the top half is 1-inch from the edge of the bottom half, forming a split-loaf shape.
7. Place on a greased baking sheet, cover with plastic wrap, and let rise again until doubled in size, about 30 minutes.
8. Bake at 375° for 40 minutes until golden brown. Cool on wire rack and sprinkle top generously with powdered sugar before serving.
Yield: 2 loaves, or about 20 servings

Limburgse vlaai
(Limburg pie)

1½ packages dry yeast
1 cup very warm water
½ tsp. sugar
2½ cups all-purpose flour
2 Tbsp. cooking oil

1. Dissolve yeast in water with sugar. Mix flour with oil and add yeast mixture, using a wooden spoon. Be sure all the flour is incorporated. This will be a sticky dough. Scrape the dough into a compact mass, cover, and let rise for about 30 minutes in a warm place.
2. Grease 2 10-inch pie pans or 4 smaller ones.
3. Using lightly floured fingers, work the dough into a ball. Divide in half and pat each half into a thick circle. Put circle of dough in each prepared pan and, using your fingers, pat and press the dough to cover the bottom of the pans. Cover and let rise in a warm place for 30 minutes.

Fillings:
4. *Fresh fruit*: Cut fruit in half and put pieces close together on dough, cut side up. Plums, peaches, and other fruits in season work well.
Canned or stewed fruit: Drain the fruit. Mix with ¼ cup sugar before filling the dough. Fill dough.
5. Bake at 400° for 30 minutes. If using fresh fruit, sprinkle with sugar 10 minutes before pies are finished.
Yield: 2 10-inch pies or 4 smaller ones

Banketletters
(almond-filled pastries)

Dough:
1 cup very cold unsalted butter (no substitutes)
2 cups all-purpose flour
½ cup cold sour cream
1 large, beaten egg yolk

1. Cut butter into small pieces and add to flour. Using a pastry blender or 2 knives, cut the butter into the flour until the butter is the size of peas. Mix sour cream with the egg yolk and blend into flour/butter mixture with a fork just until the dough forms a "ball."
2. Divide the dough into 2 pieces, wrap well, and refrigerate for several hours or days, if desired. Allow dough to come to room temperature before making cookies.

Filling:
1 8-oz. can almond paste or, to make your own:

¼ lb. blanched almonds
½ cup granulated sugar
1 large, beaten egg

3. Grind the almonds and mix with the sugar. Add the egg and, using a wooden spoon or your hands, work until smooth and manageable. The almond paste will keep well for several weeks if wrapped securely and refrigerated.

4. Roll the dough out to ⅛-inch thickness and cut dough into strips 3½ to 4-inches wide.
5. Work the almond paste into little round sticks about the length and diameter of your finger. Lay these almond paste sticks either end to end for a long cookie that may be formed into a wreath or crosswise to roll the dough around each stick individually. For sticks, cut the dough, place a dab of water under each end, and tuck under. Begin again with the next "stick." Sticks may also be formed into initials by making slits where parts of letters must join and dampening with a little water.
6. Place cookies, initials, or wreath seam side down on a cookie sheet and brush with 1 egg that has been beaten with 1 Tbsp. of water. Bake at 400° for 20-25 minutes or until golden brown. Cool on a rack. May be served warm if desired.
Yield: about 20 cookies

Oliebollen
(apple-raisin doughnuts)

1 cup milk
1 Tbsp. sugar
2 Tbsp. unsalted butter
½ tsp. salt
1 package dry yeast
½ cup very warm water
1 egg
3 cups all-purpose flour
2 cups chopped, tart apples
¾ cup dried currants or raisins
oil for deep frying
powdered sugar

1. Heat milk, sugar, butter, and salt just until warm. Dissolve yeast in warm water and add milk mixture, egg, and 1½ cups of flour. Beat until smooth.

2. Stir in apples and currants or raisins and add remaining flour to form a soft dough. Cover and let rise in a warm place until doubled in bulk, about 1 hour.
3. Drop tablespoon by tablespoon, a few at a time, into oil that has been heated to 375°. Fry until golden brown, about 5 minutes.
4. Drain on paper towels and roll in powdered sugar.
Yield: about 30 fritters

Dutch Accents

Pinwheel ornament

Assemble:
2-color heavy decorator foil
  or 2 colors lighter foil paper (gift-
  wrap is suitable), to be glued paper
  side to paper side with foil sides out
scissors
ruler
1-inch brass paper fasteners
9-inch colored pipe cleaners
white glue

1. Cut a 6-inch square from the heavy foil, using a ruler to measure. *Or*, if you use lighter foil, cut two 6-inch squares, one of each color, and work both pieces together, foil sides out. Use a dab of white glue between the points and in the center to hold the squares together.

2. Cut a diagonal line from each corner to 1-inch from center.

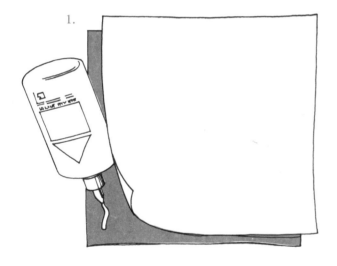

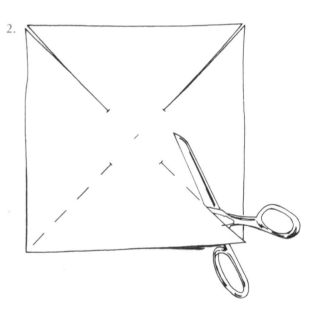

3. Take every other point and bend over center. With nail, knife, or hole punch, carefully make a small hole through the points at center. Push paper fastener through the hole from the front. Open paper fastener at back of pinwheel.

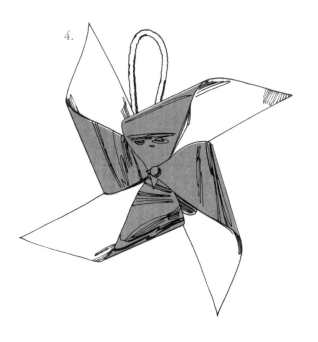

4.

4. Attach pipe cleaner to back of fastener. Hang ornament from tree with pipe cleaner. Repeat for more pinwheels.

If desired, multicolored pinwheels or patterned pinwheels may be made from several different heavy foils or light-foil combinations. If desired, use a 12-inch square to make a pinwheel ornament for the top of the tree or decoration elsewhere.

Garlands

1.

Assemble:
1 gross (144) pre-drilled silver plastic or glass beads (multifaceted ones reflect better)
3 doz. pre-drilled larger red beads
280 pre-drilled small, round, red beads
large jar lids or small bowls
quilting thread or other strong thread
needle
scissors

These instructions are for a garland approximately 8½ feet long. The number of beads available determines the length of the garland.

1. To keep beads from rolling away when working, place in jar lids or bowls. Thread needle with 72 inches of thread. Double back thread and knot, leaving a 2-inch tail or longer. *Or*, if easier for you, work with shorter lengths. All will be tied together later.

2. Pass the needle through the holes in the beads, one by one. For this pattern, use the following order: 3 small red beads, 1 silver, 2 small red, 1 silver, 3 small red, 1 silver, 1 large red, 1 silver. Repeat until the length of thread is full except for last 2¼ inches.

2.

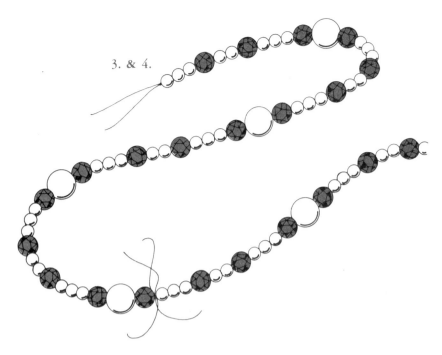

3. & 4.

3. Cut the thread at the needle and tie a knot as close to the last bead as possible, leaving a tail of at least 2 inches. Rethread needle and repeat twice (or more than twice, if using shorter lengths of thread), each time picking up the pattern where you left off. Now you have 3 lengths of garland (or more if you used shorter lengths).

4. Tie lengths of garland at the tails as closely as possible, making sure to match up pattern. Make sure knots are secure, then snip excess thread. The garland is now ready to be hung on the tree or placed elsewhere as decoration.

If desired, create your own garland patterns with different colors and shapes of beads.

Kerstkransjes
(Christmas wreath cookies)

Ingredients:
⅔ cup butter
½ cup honey
1 Tbsp. water
2¼ cups whole wheat pastry flour
 or, substitute 2½ cups all-purpose flour
1 tsp. baking powder
finely grated peel of ½ lemon
1 egg, beaten
rock sugar
 or, substitute colored sugar crystals
½ cup chopped, blanched almonds
extra flour and butter

Assemble:
measuring cups and spoons
rubber spatula
1 large and 1 small mixing bowl
electric or hand mixer
mixing spoon
food wrap
pastry board
rolling pin
drinking glass with rim 1½-inches to 3-inches in diameter
cookie sheets
thimble
knife or nut chopper
pastry brush
potholders
wire cooling rack
18-inch lengths of thin, red ribbon

1. Bring all ingredients to room temperature. In large mixing bowl, cream butter, honey, and water together with mixer until well blended.

1.

2. With spoon, mix flour, baking powder, and lemon peel together in small mixing bowl. Add a little at a time to butter/honey mixture, mixing continually. Knead until mixture forms a soft ball, adding more flour, if necessary. Chill dough in food wrap for at least 1 hour.

For 2-inch cookies:

3. Preheat oven to 375°. On floured board, roll half the dough out to ⅛-inch thickness. Cut out circles with glass. Cut out centers with thimble to create cookie wreaths. Reserve centers to make more cookies.

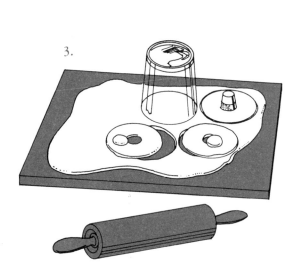

4. Place cookies on buttered cookie sheet, about 1-inch apart. Lightly brush cookies with beaten egg and sprinkle with sugar and chopped almonds. Bake cookies for about 8 minutes, or until golden brown. (Length of cooking will increase and decrease with size of cookie desired.) Begin preparing second half of dough while first batch bakes. Remove cookies from oven and cool on sheet until no longer soft. Remove to wire rack to cool completely.

5. Tie the cooled cookies to the tree with lengths of red ribbon, one length for each cookie. Children may remove wreath cookies from tree as Christmas treats.

Yield: about 6 dozen 2-inch cookie wreaths

Painted walnuts

Assemble:
walnuts in the shell
hinge-type nutcracker or butter knife
beading wire, or very thin wire
scissors
white glue
wire cooling rack
4 tall glasses of equal height
nontoxic tempera poster paints
small paint brushes
ornament hangers or string

1. Carefully crack each walnut into 2 unbroken halves, using nutcracker or butter knife. Remove the nutmeats and set aside for baking or eating.
2. Cut a 6-inch piece of wire. Twist the ends together to form a loop. Tuck twisted end of loop into end of one walnut-shell half. Put a thin coat of glue on the edge of the other walnut-shell half and fit the 2 halves back together. Dry thoroughly. Repeat for each walnut.
3. On a level surface, set wire cooling rack on top of glasses, one glass at each corner.
4. Holding a walnut by wire, paint desired color. With ornament hanger or string suspend walnut from wire rack to dry. Repeat with other walnuts, arranging them on rack so weight of ornaments is evenly distributed.

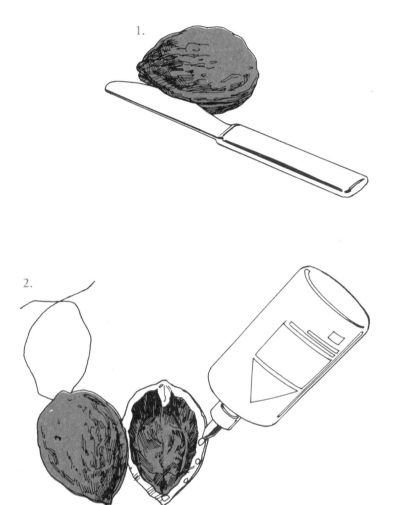

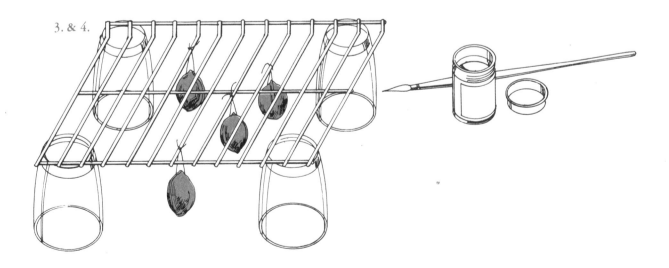

5. When completely dry, hang walnuts from tree.

If desired, other types of nuts may be painted in the same fashion for use as ornaments. For variety, glitter may be applied to painted nuts while still wet in order to produce a sparkle effect.

5.

Dutch Melodies

Look, There Is the Steamer
(Zie Ginds Komt de Stoomboot)

Adagio   Traditional

1. Look, there is the steam-er from far a-way lands. It
Zie ginds komt de stoom-boot uit Span-je weer aan. Hij

brings us St. Nich'las, he's waving his hands. His horse is a-pranc-ing on
brengt ons Sint Niklaas ik zie hem al staan. Hoe hup-pelt zijn paard-je het

deck, up and down, The ban-ners are wa-ving in vil-lage and town.
dek op en neer, Hoe waai-en de wim-pels al heen en al weer.

2. Black Peter is laughing
   And tells everyone,
   "The good kids get candy,
   The bad kids get none!"
   Oh, please, dear St. Nicholas,
   If Pete and you would,
   Just visit our house
   For we all have been good.

Nicholas, I Beg of You
(Sinterklaas Kapoentje)

Moderato

Traditional

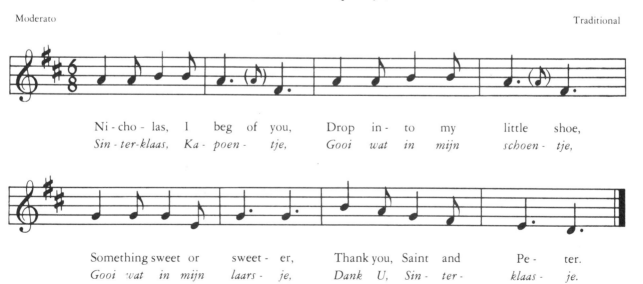

Ni-cho-las, I beg of you, Drop in-to my little shoe,
Sin-ter-klaas, Ka-poen-tje, Gooi wat in mijn schoen-tje,

Something sweet or sweet-er, Thank you, Saint and Pe-ter.
Gooi wat in mijn laars-je, Dank U, Sin-ter-klaas-je.

Good Saint Nicholas
(*Sint Niklaasje Kom Maar Binnen*)

Allegretto

Traditional

Good St. Nich'las is in Holland once a - gain With his horse and Peter from
Sint Ni - klaasje kom maar bin-nen met je knecht, En we zit- ten al - le - maal

sun - ny Spain. And e - ven if he can't stay long, We hope he'll
e - ven recht, Mis - schien heeft u wel e - ven tijd, Voor u

stop to hear our song. Dear St. Ni - cho - las the door is o-pen
weer naar Span - je rijdt. Sint Ni - klaasje kom maar e - ven bij ons

wide, For you and Pete to step in - side. And we're singing, voices
aan, Maar laat uw schim- mel bui- ten staan. En we zin-gen en we

ringing, and our hearts re - joice 'Cause the saint loves all good girls and boys.
springen en we zijn zo blij, Want er zijn geen stou - te kind'- ren bij.

Bright December Moon

(Zie de Maan Schijnt)

Andante Traditional

Bright De - cem - ber moon is beam- ing, Boys and girls now stop your play! For to-
Zie de maan schijnt door de bo - men, Mak-kers staakt uw wild ge - raas! 't Heerlijk

night's the wondrous eve - ning, Eve of good St. Nicholas Day. O'er the
a - vondj' is ge - ko - men, 't A-vond - je van Sin - ter - klaas. Vol ver -

roofs his horse un - shod, Brings us gifts or else the rod.
wach - ting klopt ons hart, Wie de koek krijgt wie de gard.

O'er the roofs his horse un- shod, Brings us gifts or else the rod.
Vol ver - wach - ting klopt ons hart, Wie de koek krijgt wie de gard.

A Little Child Is Born

(Er Is een Kindeke Geboren)

Andante con moto

Traditional

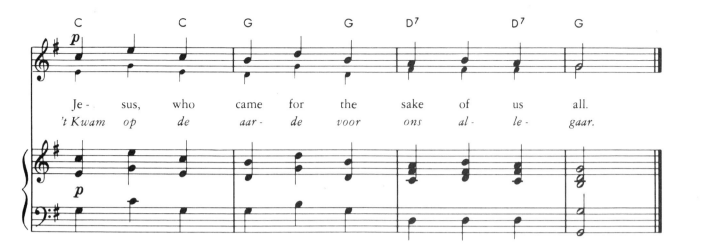

Je - sus, who came for the sake of us all.
't Kwam op de aar - de voor ons al - le - gaar.

2. Beneath his tiny head no pillow but hay,
   God's richest treasure in rude manger lay.

3. His eyes of blackest jet were sparkling with light,
   Rosy cheeks bloomed on his face fair and bright.

4. And from his lovely mouth, the laughter did swell,
   When he saw Mary, whom he loved so well.

5. He came to weary earth, so dark and so drear,
   To wish to mankind a blessed New Year.

Acknowledgments

Cover: © Kees van den Berg, Photo Researchers

2: Universal News Organization

6: Bettmann Archive, Inc.

7: Netherlands Information Service

8: FIBO-Beeldonderwijs B. V. from Image Finders

9: National Foto-Persbureau B. V. (Netherlands Information Service)

10: (Top) FIBO-Beeldonderwijs B. V. from Image Finders
(Bottom) Articapress

11: © Claude Lévesque (Entreprise Int. de Photographie)

12–13: FIBO-Beeldonderwijs B. V. from Image Finders

13: Peter Borsboom

15: (Top) © Spaarnestad B. V.
(Bottom) © Fotographie Marcel Minnée

16: © Claude Lévesque (Entreprise Int. de Photographie)

18: Karel Hofland

19: © Spaarnestad B. V.

20: Rijksmuseum, Amsterdam

21: Fotostudio Rimi Jansen (Bedrijfschap Banketbakkersbedrijf)

22: © Claude Lévesque (Entreprise Int. de Photographie)

23: © Kees van den Berg, Photo Researchers

24: Bedrijfschap Banketbakkersbedrijf
(Insert) © Kees van den Berg, Photo Researchers

25: © Claude Lévesque (Entreprise Int. de Photographie)

26: (Top) © Kees van den Berg, Photo Researchers
(Bottom) WORLD BOOK photo by Steve Hale

29: (Top) FIBO-Beeldonderwijs B. V. from Image Finders
(Bottom) FIBO-Beeldonderwijs B. V. from Image Finders

30: FIBO-Beeldonderwijs B. V. from Image Finders

31: © Spaarnestad B. V.

32: (Left) Peter Borsboom
(Right) © Claude Lévesque (Entreprise Int. de Photographie)

33: Peter Borsboom

34: Peter Borsboom

35: (Top) FIBO-Beeldonderwijs B. V. from Image Finders
(Bottom) © Claude Lévesque (Entreprise Int. de Photographie)

36: (Top left) © Kees van den Berg, Photo Researchers

(Top right) Peter Borsboom
(Bottom) © Kees van den Berg, Photo Researchers

37: (Top) © Kees van den Berg, Photo Researchers
(Bottom) Peter Borsboom

38: Verkeersburo Stichting VVV Friesland-Leeuwarden

39: Peter Borsboom

40: The Granger Collection

41: © Spaarnestad B. V.

42: (Left) Articapress (Netherlands Information Service)
(Right) Articapress (Netherlands Information Service)

43: Peter Borsboom

44: (Top) Articapress (Royal Netherlands Embassy)
(Bottom) Carole Graham

45: © Spaarnestad B. V.

46: © Claude Lévesque (Entreprise Int. de Photographie)

47: (Top) © Spaarnestad B. V.
(Bottom) © Spaarnestad B. V.

49: Ir. W. F. v. Heemskerck Düker (Royal Netherlands Embassy)

50: The Granger Collection

51: Peter Borsboom

52: Peter Borsboom

53: (Top) © Claude Lévesque (Entreprise Int. de Photographie)
(Bottom) Peter Borsboom (Royal Netherlands Embassy)

54: (Top) © Kees van den Berg, Photo Researchers
(Bottom) © Spaarnestad B. V.

55: Theater Zuidplein

56: Royal Netherlands Embassy

57: © Fotographie Marcel Minnée

58: The Granger Collection

59: Peter Borsboom (Royal Netherlands Embassy)

60: Frisian Tourist Office VVV

61: © Claude Lévesque (Entreprise Int. de Photographie)

62: (Top) Articapress
(Bottom) © Claude Lévesque (Entreprise Int. de Photographie)

63: © Spaarnestad B. V.

64: WORLD BOOK photo by Steve Hale

65: The Granger Collection

68–73: James Curran

74–77: William Chin